BOOS

Dr Eamonn Butler is   ......am Smith
Institute, a leading policy think-tank based in
London. A former R. C. Hoiles Distinguished
Scholar and with degrees in psychology, eco-
nomics and philosophy from the University of
St Andrews, Dr Butler is author of three
books about the work of Nobel Prizewinning
economists and co-author of Pan's *Test Your
IQ*.

Dr Madsen Pirie is Secretary of British Mensa,
the high-IQ society. He was Distinguished
Visiting Professor of Philosophy and Logic at
Hillsdale College, Michigan, and is currently
President of the Adam Smith Instiute in London.
He is author of *The Book of the Fallacy*,
Privatization, and *Micropolitics*, and co-author
of Pan's *Test Your IQ*.

EAMONN BUTLER
and
MADSEN PIRIE

BOOST YOUR IQ

A Pan Original
PAN BOOKS
London, Sydney and Auckland

ACKNOWLEDGEMENTS

Special thanks are owed to our friends Harold Gale, the Executive Director of Mensa, and Victor Serebriakoff, the President of Mensa. Thanks go also to all the Mensans who participated in our tests and who helped with suggestions and advice.

Readers who are interested in joining Mensa, the high-IQ society, should write for details to Mensa, Freepost, Wolverhampton.

Dr Eamonn Butler
Dr Madsen Pirie

First published in 1990 by Pan Books Ltd
Cavaye Place, London SW10 9PG

9 8 7 6 5 4 3 2 1

© Eamonn Butler and Madsen Pirie 1990

ISBN 0 330 30728 2

Typeset by Macmillan Production Limited

Printed in England by Clays Ltd, St Ives plc

CONTENTS

PART FOUR: RE-TEST YOUR IQ

PART FIVE: ANSWERS

HOW THIS BOOK WORKS

This book gives you practical coaching on IQ test questions. It should help build up your understanding of how IQ tests work and your confidence in being able to do them.

It is divided into five parts.

PART ONE is demystification. It fills in some of the background about what IQ tests are supposed to measure, how useful they are, and the arguments that have raged about them. You will never be in awe of IQ tests again.

PART TWO contains a typical test which is designed to give a quick estimate of your IQ so you can see the starting point from which you want to give yourself a boost. Before the test comes a series of instructions about how to test yourself.

Don't cheat yourself by looking through the questions or the answers; if you are to gain a realistic assessment of the progress you have made through reading this book, you should come at all the questions afresh.

PART THREE is the coaching section that will help you to boost your IQ. Some typical sorts of question that are quite commonly used in IQ tests are picked out, stripped down, and analysed. Once you understand how they work and what IQ testers seek from them, you will be able to toy with a few of the other examples that are given and build up your confidence and understanding to the maximum.

Among the broad types of question that are covered will be:

Number questions (numerical ability)
Words and letters (verbal ability)
Mixtures of numbers, words, and letters

Diagram questions (visuo-spatial ability)
Logic puzzles

The section closes with some last-minute hints on general test-taking technique which you may find useful when facing any kind of examination, not just an IQ test.

PART FOUR provides another test of roughly the same difficulty as the first. You can check your score against the first test and see how successfully you have boosted your IQ!

The answers to all the test and exercise questions can be found in PART FIVE at the back of the book. No peeking! — That will make it impossible to check how much progress you have made.
Good luck!

PART ONE

IQ AND
IQ TESTING

CHAPTER ONE

BOOSTING YOUR IQ

Is it really possible to boost your IQ?

The answer is *yes*. And that is despite most people's belief that their IQ is like their date of birth – an unchangeable statistic which they escape only when they go on to meet the great intelligence tester in the sky.

To earthbound psychologists, the concept of intelligence is far less solid. They are not sure what it is at all. The only thing they are reasonably confident about is that intelligence tests measure it. Sort of. Roughly.

That is great news to the aspiring IQ booster, because if you can improve your score on intelligence tests – *and you can* – nobody has any right to call you a bonehead again. Particularly the psychologists who devise the tests and conduct the interviews for the job vacancies and the college places.

You can beat them at their own game just by understanding how they think about intelligence and construct their tests. Discover the knack of boosting your test score and they will have to admit you are intelligent.

INTELLIGENCE AND IQ TESTS

'Intelligence is what intelligence tests measure.'

That is what the cornered psychologist will say when faced with an angry mob demanding to know what intelligence is. And, you know, the poor creature has a point.

It is the sort of maxim that looks very odd to the layman, of course. But scientists have no difficulty with such definitions and regularly toy with at least six over breakfast. To them there are plenty of concepts that can be discussed and defined only in terms of how you measure them.

The point is that intelligence is in the mind of the beholder. Saying that someone is 'bright' or 'dim', 'sharp' or 'dull' is just our way of sifting their behaviour into some semblance of order that we find manageable and helpful. There aren't bits of brightness and dimness littered around, waiting to be *discovered*; they are just conceptual pigeon-holes that we *invent* to distinguish different people in some useful way.

The trouble with scientists is that they are never happy with having only two pigeon-holes and always want a whole row of them, preferably with official-looking numbers by the side. That is how they end up with scales of measurement by which they can separate people even more exquisitely.

But like all filing systems, these scales are quite arbitrary. If you are trying to describe your concept of temperature, it doesn't matter whether you use Fahrenheit or Centigrade scales; if you are trying to organize your library, it is up to you whether you employ the Dewey or the Library of Congress filing systems; and there is nothing very magical about the IQ scale either.

It is only after you have sorted your library into some order that you can review its relative strengths and weaknesses, its subject gaps and overlaps. You can maintain that today is warmer than yesterday only if you refer to some temperature scale. And you can discuss intelligence only in terms of how you measure that, too.

That is where intelligence testing comes in.

WHAT SORT OF TEST?

Library cataloguers know that there are umpteen places you might put the same book, especially if it covers a range of different subjects. Then new scientific subjects come in and burgeon, demanding whole new catalogue sections and subsections to themselves, while old subjects fade from fashion and might just as well be lumped together under a smaller heading. There is no right or wrong way of doing it, you just have to devise some system that works reasonably well. There is a large measure of agreement about the general principles that are best to use, but plenty of argument about the details, sometimes about important details.

Just as the rules by which the librarian decides how to catalogue a particular book are not always clear, psychologists have the same doubts about how best to test and classify people in terms of intelligence.

Should it be the *difficulty* of the problems people can solve, or the *range* of different problems, or what? And if somebody is good at one sort of test – number puzzles, for example – and bad at others – such as word puzzles – how should they be judged against people with the reverse capabilities?

Not surprisingly, there are disputes about how intelligence tests should be put together and how they should set about examining whatever it is that they try to measure.

The academic fisticuffs have been going on since the late Victorian age. The physical punch-ups started more recently: Professor Hans Eysenck in Britain and Professor Arthur Jensen in the United States are only two of the prominent academics who have received bloody noses for their views on intelligence, from student activists who seemingly thought them mistaken.

BOOST YOUR IQ

As an aspiring IQ booster you do not need to worry too much about these arguments, though it helps to know which of the factions in the squabble set the test you are about to take because the questions will be different.

And if you understand all these points about IQ testing, at least you know that you don't have to change your inner nature in some way. You just have to be good at tests.

That won't make you a better person, or guarantee you fame and success in life; but it might help you to get chosen for things and enjoy some opportunities you might miss otherwise. As they say of sincerity, once you can fake that, you've got it made.

It's not exactly a case of faking your score on intelligence tests, but you can certainly do a few things to improve it. This book should teach you a few tricks of the trade so that you will get a better score on IQ tests – perhaps a score which more accurately reflects your mental abilities today than that old-fashioned IQ test you did so badly on as a kid in school.

CHAPTER TWO

FAMILIARITY AND PERFORMANCE

Intelligence tests have been around a long time. The first really extensive use of them was in the First World War, when military commanders found it useful to have some scientific-looking way of deciding who should give orders to dig the trenches and who should do the digging.

Tests are still used today for much the same purposes. New recruits going into the army almost anywhere in the developed world will find themselves taking an IQ test of some description. It helps discipline if military commanders can find some way of justifying the way they allocate other ranks to their various unpleasant duties.

From this, however, two things follow.

CAUTION IN THE RANKS

First, beware of those neat charts which suggest a strong correlation between a person's IQ and what he ends up doing in his professional adult life.

Of course, it is quite right that we do indeed find generals and professors, for example, clustering at the top end of the IQ range, while private soldiers and road sweepers tend to be found at the bottom. And one explanation might well be that the exacting demands of the top professions mean that only the brainiest people can get along in them. It probably does help to have something between the ears if you intend to be a professor or a field marshal (although there have certainly been quite a few celebrated exemplars who didn't).

On the other hand, this neat correlation might be only the bottom line of a self-fulfilling prophecy. The whizz-kid psychologists who give all the recruits a brain test on day one will undoubtedly assign the high-IQ recruits to the fast-track training courses that open the door to promotion, and then book everyone else in for square-bashing. So it is only those with the highest IQ (or the very best family connections) who get considered for the top jobs.

Whereupon the psychologists, and a few other souls who believe that IQ is 90% of success in life (being nice to the boss's secretary accounts for the other 10%) smile smugly and say 'told you so'.

FAMILIARITY

The second, more important point is that most people today are reasonably familiar with the concept of an IQ test and in many countries it could be that a majority have taken one at some time in their lives. And that does affect the results.

People living in countries with compulsory national service in the armed forces, or where there is a selective schools system and a college aptitude examination, will surely have encountered an intelligence test of some sort. The First World War soldiers could not have been prepared for the mysterious squiggles, sums, and series which were meted out to them; those same symbols (or at least, their modern descendants) are far more familiar to people today.

This is not altogether good news for the intending IQ booster because some modern intelligence testers try to compensate a little for that. They work on the presentation of their questions so that the tests look just as odd as they did in 1914.

At the same time, however, the widespread use of IQ tests and their apparent usefulness in selection procedures means that there are many different sorts of test in circulation. The practised IQ booster knows that it is worth asking what sort of test you are being invited to do. If you can't get on with that sort – if you are hopeless at language or mathematical questions, for example – why not check if one using picture questions is available and equally acceptable for the test purposes?

CRACKING THE CODE

In any event, no matter how cunningly the modern intelligence testers might present their material, the trick lies in breaking the code. If you have learnt beforehand the range of codes which IQ testers tend to use, then it becomes easier to get a good score.

It is a little bit like those cryptic crossword puzzles you see in the newspapers. Code words appear in the clues: thus 'congressman deranged . . . ' (or 'inverted' or 'confused') means that the answer is an anagram of 'congressman'; the word 'point' or 'pole' or 'cardinal' in a clue can often mean that the answer contains one of the compass-points N,S,E, or W in it; 'sailor' or 'tar' indicates the presence of the letter sequence AB, the standard abbreviation for Able Seaman; and so on . Know the code, and you can do the crossword – or do it much more speedily.

And speed is important in modern IQ tests.

It used to be that intelligence tests were given by individual testers to individual candidates. That was due partly to the type of material included which could not be presented and assessed in any other way. So for the majority of questions, the time factor was unimportant.

Nowadays, however, there is a demand for IQ tests that can be given to large groups of people, so the tests have to be straight forward to administer, quick to do, and speedily marked.

That puts a strain on the IQ test designer, who will want to give candidates a fairly wide mixture of different intelligence tasks in the half-hour or so set aside for the test. (So no matter how unfamiliar the question looks, if it takes a long time to solve, you've probably got it wrong.)

The experienced taker of IQ tests knows therefore that the composer of the test is not likely to set convoluted questions requiring lengthy mental peregrinations, which in turn means that there are not all that many codes available to the tester. If you know how to crack most of them and can speed through the easier questions, you will have a reasonable IQ score under your belt right away.

CHAPTER THREE

GETTING TO THE ROOTS OF IQ

SORTING OUT HUMAN NATURE

If you were doing a historical survey about where the concept of intelligence comes from, the chances are that you would start with the Greek philosopher Plato. However, the ancient Greeks did not really conceptualize the human mind and personality as we would think about it today.

Nonetheless, there were some interesting efforts to get to grips with the problem. Plato suggested that our nature, what he called 'the soul', is divided into three pieces: the appetites (such as hunger or thirst); reason (like when you are gasping for a drink, but don't take one because you know that the local water is thick with bacteria); and 'spirit' (something like what we would call a sense of honour or propriety).

This is called by philosophers the 'tripartite division of the soul', and by students (reflecting perhaps on Plato's totalitarian vision of society) the 'tri-apartheid division of the soul'.

EARLY OCCUPATIONAL PSYCHOLOGY

So it is true that the ancient thinkers made at least some sort of distinction between reasoning processes and the force of desires, passions, feelings, and emotions.

You could even make a case for Plato being the world's first occupational psychologist. He thought you might divide humankind as a whole into three categories as well, and that the top jobs would be given to those of the best mettle (or metal, since the division depended on whether you were a 'gold', 'silver', or 'bronze' person). The assignment would be made at birth, which squashes the ideas of any softies who think that upbringing might be important. Plato and his chums would be all right, of course, coming from good families.

Still, it was not exactly clear to the Greeks how one might assess personal abilities or what should be included in any scrutiny. That is probably just as well because upper-class snobs like Aristotle (another one to ponder the subject) would regard the ability to manage your country estate to be far more important than the ability to think your way out of bed in the morning.

INTERVENING CENTURIES

Not a great deal of further thought was devoted to the subject until well through the nineteenth century. Partly this was because other things were thought to be more important than the study of intelligence – not getting mixed up in the Hundred Years War, getting on with the business of inventing machines to take the work out of agriculture and industry, and so on.

Even in the eighteenth and nineteenth centuries there seemed to prevail a view that most people were pretty much the same in terms of ability, though there were a few village idiots and a few men of genius (women, of course, would not qualify), and that was that. So what was there to discuss?

Thomas Arnold put intelligence in its place in his *Address to his Scholars at Rugby*:

> What we must look for here is, first, religious and moral principles; secondly, gentlemanly conduct; thirdly, intellectual ability.

IQ IN THE AGE OF SCIENCE

Herbert Spencer, exploring the ramifications of the new-found theories of Charles Darwin, concluded that reasoning ability was probably far more important than religious principles and gentlemanly conduct when it came to deciding which species would make it through the selective process. The ability to spot important things, to work out how they fit together, and to apply that understanding to the task in hand – no matter what the task might be – would be the key to survival. Suddenly the subject became interesting.

Sir Francis Galton was also groping towards the idea that some sort of general mental ability might be separated out from people's particular gifts for specific tasks. He attempted, rather unsuccessfully, to discover whether people did consistently well on mental tasks, and whether this might be linked to physical and other characteristics.

For example, he suggested that people with great mental ability showed a particular acuity in the discrimination of fine differences in weight. It could be that all the brainy people he met were fellow scientists who specialized in weighing out *avoirdupois* measures of various chemicals and got to be quite good at it. (Then again, fish merchants are pretty good at judging pounds and ounces, which may or may not have confirmed his theories.)

Other people looked around in vain for other links between mental ability – or at least, academic performance – and physical features such as eyesight, colour vision, hearing, reaction time, sensitivity to pain, mental imagery and even colour preferences. Alfred Binet thought he discovered some link between school performance and memory (which does not seem all that surprising). Another Frenchman, T. Simon, thought it possible to distinguish profoundly retarded children from merely backward ones by checking the number of glances at the page it took them to copy out a few phrases of writing.

INTO THE TWENTIETH CENTURY

These researches were crude but systematic attempts to find some simple way to measure mental abilities. IQ testing proper, though, started around the turn of the century.

In fact it was Alfred Binet who first devised an IQ scale, designed for use on children and based on the idea of a 'mental age' which is no longer used today but which still haunts people's conceptions of what IQ is all about. Then, on a governmental assignment, Binet and Simon devised a series of tests to discover which Parisian children would be mentally unable to benefit much from the traditional schooling system.

Today, those tests look rather feeble. The tests required knowledge rather than intelligence and because they relied on spoken answers or on the observed proficiency with which the children could copy words and pictures, they could be given only to one child at a time.

Nevertheless, those efforts did stimulate some further thought about what IQ tests should try to test and how they could be designed for use on large groups of people.

ALL-ROUND ABILITY

Also emerging was the view that these various testing programmes did indeed reveal some links. They were not the expected correlations between physical attributes (strength, speed, etc.) and academic performance, however. Rather it was that people who did well on one sort of mental task (memory, for example) could be expected to do pretty well on other sorts (such as the ability to copy complicated patterns) as well.

As a result there arose the concept of general mental ability: that people possessed a global intellectual ability that helped them on just about any mental task they turned to.

Debate in the early years of the twentieth century centred around this question of whether there was indeed some sort of all-round mental ability that helped you to perform well on almost any reasoning task, or whether different sorts of task (involving words, numbers, diagrams, or memory) really did demand several different sorts of special mental ability which people would possess in different mixtures.

The principal protagonists in the debate were the psychologists Charles Spearman of London and L. L. Thurstone of Chicago. The outcome agreed at the time was that both views contained some truth. One individual might be good at numerical tasks, bad at visual ones, while another might show precisely the opposite pattern. Nevertheless, lump them all together and we discover statistically that people who do well on one sort of reasoning task still tend to do well on others.

In other words, your gift for figures or words is important, but your general mental ability is important too. It just depends on which you need most at the time.

THE LEGACY IN IQ TESTS

Over the years, this cosy agreement has been attacked with various degrees of passion and amended with various degrees of commitment.

Psychologists in need of guinea-pigs have a habit of using their research students, schoolboys, or the residents of the local psychiatric hospital – all of which are conveniently to hand, but each of which is about as representative of humankind as the average laboratory rat and his lawyer. Intellectually beating up the design of the experiment is only one way of dispelling any scientific consensus about reasoning abilities, and there are other methods too.

Despite these wrangles, the basic view emerging from the Spearman-Thurstone episode shapes perhaps the bulk of intelligence testing today. It explains, for example, why tests employ reasoning tasks, designed to get at general mental ability and presented in mathematical, verbal, visuo-spatial and other formats, the formats designed to reflect a spread of special mental abilities. Whatever the rights and wrongs of that compromise, it is a long way from the simple tests of acquired knowledge and copying ability pioneered by Binet and Simon.

CHAPTER FOUR

THE DESIGN OF IQ TESTS

The debate about whether people possess some general mental ability that helps them on all reasoning tasks, or a series of special abilities for particular types of task, is instructive. It reveals some of the difficulties involved in approaching the elusive concept of general reasoning ability.

We cannot get inside heads to measure intelligence directly, so we have to devise a test. But for a candidate to get the right answer on any particular item in that test might involve a whole range of factors – special ability on the type of question, memory skills, and knowledge acquired through life, for example. Yet these are indirect and perhaps poor indicators of any underlying reasoning ability.

KNOWLEDGE AND INTELLIGENCE

Although IQ tests might seek to discover the abstract form of this mental ability, those other factors inevitably intervene. Any IQ test ends up checking some combination of acquired knowledge, special abilities, and general intelligence.

One thing which tests routinely assume, for instance, is that candidates know enough of their native language to understand what they are being asked to do on each question. Of course there is some link between that and intelligence, because profoundly retarded people may not have learnt much useful language; but the acquired knowledge of a language is not the same as intelligence.

Perhaps Albert Wiggam was correct when he wrote that intelligence is the thing that enables people to get along without education, while education enables people to get along without using their intelligence.

Still, questions involving words, or alphabetical sequences, or simple numerical operations – the very stuff of modern mass-production IQ tests – do presume that these routine things have already been learnt by the candidate. The degree to which past learning helps you varies from question to question, but it is always there. The worry is not *whether* IQ tests confuse knowledge and intelligence but *how much* they do.

As soon as this issue was recognized, people started designing 'culture-fair' test items that (hopefully) would owe much more to abstract reasoning ability than to acquired knowledge. Part of the idea was to invent tests that could compare the intelligence of people from different countries, even though they might not share the same sort of general background knowledge. But we can never isolate the two things completely.

CULTURE-FAIR AND CULTURE-BOUND TESTS

It is not too difficult to imagine test questions that depend a lot on background knowledge. Take these items, for example:

CULTURE-BOUND QUESTIONS

I Spot the odd one out:

Beethoven Tchaikovsky Britten Disraeli Mozart

2 Archeology is the study of:

Architecture Aristocrats Antiquities Arches Artists

3 Guernica is to Picasso as Sunflower is to:

Titian Newton Van Gogh Aristotle
Gainsborough Stalin

4 Threat means nearly the same as:

Blackmail Anger Fear Worry Menace Disturb

5 Underline the right word to complete the sentence:

He (swimmed, swam, swum) across the river.

6 I started the day with £1 2s 6d in my pocket. I spent 2/6d
on fish and chips, 6d on ice-cream, and 3/- on fairground
rides. How much was I left with?

Questions of these general shapes – odd one out, definitions, relationships, synonyms, arithmetic – might be found in nearly every
general IQ test you can pick up. But they require a good deal of
background knowledge of painting, music, science, and nuances in
the language itself. The £sd arithmetic, which was at one time a
fairly routine sort of question in the UK and Commonwealth countries such as Canada and Australia, looks very strange today: but
the other questions would be no less odd and no less difficult to
someone brought up in a non-Western culture.

If you have been to a nice school in the West, you should get by
easily enough, and come up with the correct answers: Disraeli,
Antiquities, Van Gogh, Menace, swam and 16/6d. But people from
countries or backgrounds where there are better things to do than
bone up on Western art, music, and numismatology cannot be
expected to perform quite so well.

So should we consign all culture-bound tests to the dustbin?
Not on your nellie. They can really be very useful, particularly on a
group of roughly similar folk. People in one country seeking a particular job probably do share much the same family and school
backgrounds, so some common knowledge can be assumed. And
in such situations we may in fact want a test that explores not only
their abstract reasoning ability, but how far they can and do use it in
picking up the particular information and techniques they will need
on the job.

Culture-fair tests, for their part, might still have to rely on some
background knowledge, but it can be quite small. Enough language
to understand the questions, a bit of counting, and a knowledge of
the alphabet should get you by on most. Some typical 'culture-fair'
questions are given by Hans Eysenck in the book he co-authored,
Intelligence: Battle for the Mind (Pan 1981). The following ones
illustrate the point.

CULTURE-FAIR(ISH) QUESTIONS

1 Complete the following series:

         1   10   17   22   25   ___

2 What should be the next letter?

         C   F   I   L   O   R   ___

3 Insert the missing word:

         TROT   (TRAP)   APEX
         CLAP   (....)   OGLE

4 Which of the numbered figures completes the sentence?

5 Complete the following sentence:

  The sky is blue and the sun _____ brightly.

6 Which of the numbered figures will complete the pattern?

The answers are 26, U, CLOG, 2, shines, and 4. In this sort of test there are certainly language questions: however, they are not designed to test the nuances of grammar and spelling, but rather the test-taker's comprehension of the sentence (in question 5) and ability to do simple letter-transformations (in question 3). Furthermore, they are questions which could be translated pretty well, unlike the language question in the previous batch of questions, which means that they should be fair to people of different linguistic backgrounds.

The sort of problem posed in question 6, in particular, is thought to be just about as culture-fair as you can get. That is why MENSA often gives applicants for membership a test comprising *only* such 'matrix' questions, devised by the distinguished psychologist D. C. Raven. As an international society, MENSA needs a test that is even-handed across cultural divides and, since the sole criterion for membership is a high IQ rather than urbanity and sophistication, that test hits its target well.

Not even this test can be completely indiscriminate, of course. The majority of Waika tribesmen in the Upper Orinoco region live in dense jungle and have probably never seen a straight line in their lives, so asking them to perform mental gymnastics with such a novelty might well put them at a disadvantage against the tribesmen of Upper Manhattan who are much more used to the everyday straight edges of bricks, walls, windows, streets and tables. Still, some of the latter may never have seen a curved line in their lives, so perhaps it's an even match.

Some Muslims, too, sometimes have difficulty on matrix questions because their cultural background does not rely much on pictorial representation. And probably the same would be true of a number of pre-literate cultures.

Other people get the right pattern, but what educated Westerners would regard as the wrong answer. One psychologist discovered that poor children in Venezuela, when asked to copy the simple diagram illustrated on the left in the figure on page 20, sometimes came up with the one on the right, but were still certain their answer was a good one:

Same, or different? Perhaps it depends on your culture

By and large, though, testers rely heavily on the matrix question because it is as reasonably culture-fair as we are ever likely to get. Another prominent psychologist, R. B. Cattell, produced another test of quite a different sort which MENSA often uses. It relies on quite a bit more background knowledge than the matrix test; however, by employing different sorts of numerical, verbal, and visual questions, it may give a better picture of all-round mental ability than a test relying on one sort of question that not everyone can get to grips with.

STANDARDIZATION AND 'GOOD' TESTS

From just these few remarks about the balance of specific abilities which people have, and the different sorts of test questions that are used, it must be getting obvious that different IQ tests cannot be regarded as measuring exactly the same thing.

How then can we tell a good test from a bad one? As in many attempts at scientific measurement, it comes down to whether the results of one type are generally consistent with the results of others. So we give large groups of people a number of different tests and see if those who tend to score well on one also tend to score well on others. If there is broad agreement in the results, then the tests are acceptable. If one test is idiosyncratic, we reject it, or use it only for specific purposes where the idiosyncrasy turns out to be a useful benefit, or wait for its inventor to convince us that his or her test is better than everyone else's.

But just as children in the school science lab know that the measurement they obtain on some experiment is never the round figure specified in the textbooks, but depends upon the state of the equipment they use, so do psychologists know that their various test equipment produces different results as well.

So agreement is unlikely to break out just yet. In the same way that we might calibrate a newly-made thermometer by looking at the temperatures indicated by an old one and then marking out the new scale accordingly, so are new IQ tests checked against the old ones. Fair enough, if we insist on having a numerical scale. But, unfortunately, when we use this procedure, the errors and biases contained in the old tests just tend to rumble on from one generation of tests to the next. The early tests were designed for educated Westerners. Some people say that any test, even a supposedly culture-fair one, which is standardized in the traditional manner merely checks everyone else against the peculiar abilities of the educated Westerner. No wonder most other cultural groups don't do so well.

The debate streams on and so, probably, will the bloody noses.

CHAPTER FIVE

MENTAL TASKS AND MENTAL TESTS

Although tests making use of acquired knowledge are valuable for many purposes, psychologists are agreed that it is not this old, received, or learnt information they want to assess with IQ tests. It is rather the ability of individuals to generate something *new* which they seek to measure.

GENERATING NEW KNOWLEDGE

According to Spearman, back in the 1920s, that ability depended on three elements.

First was the power to apprehend experience – to notice what goes on in the world and in the person's own mind.

Then comes the 'eduction of relations'. That is, when faced with two or more items, how easily do you work out any relationship between them? What, for example, fills the 'relation' space in the following illustration?

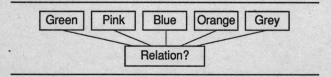

Along with this is the 'eduction of correlates'. That means, if you start with some item you have observed, and have in mind some relationship, you can work out what the associated item or items might be. To illustrate the point, think what completes this pattern:

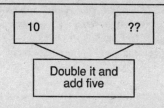

Classic IQ tests put these notions to work. In most questions you will have to detect the relation between a number of different elements and, having done that, work out which further item would follow on.

Take for instance the simple numerical question:

Q: What number is next in the series?

          1   2   4   8   __

Here you have to work out the relationship between one number and the next – that they double each time – and then work out what is the double of eight to get the answer, 16. IQ testers pride themselves on finding new and unusual ways of getting you to do much the same series of steps. IQ boosters pride themselves on seeing through the camouflage.

COMPLEXITY

Of course, the relation might be much less simple than mere doubling or mere addition. There may be lots of different items that have to be taken together before a pattern can be discerned. And by and large, people with higher IQs can solve complex problems with more facility than other people.

There may be some complex problems which people of below-average intelligence would never solve in a year. But many IQ test questions are a bit like chess puzzles – most players can solve them eventually but grand masters can usually see the answer straight away. If we gave people unlimited time to think about the questions on an IQ test, we might see quite a number of perfect scores, but that would not tell us much. So all but a few IQ tests are against the clock, using questions of only modest complexity that can be done quickly.

Too great a spread of question difficulty on a test is not very convenient for the testers anyway. The easiest way to score an IQ test is just to add up the number of rights and wrongs, then translate that into an IQ score. But then, if there is a great diversity of difficulty, you have to work out ways of giving extra credit to candidates who get all the difficult ones right even though they might get the easy ones wrong (or not attempt them). The candidate who fails all the hard ones but does all the easier ones should presumably not receive a higher IQ score just because of getting a larger number of questions right.

Still, that is a sophistication rarely seen on most published IQ tests that are designed for easy use. So the quicker you work, the higher you are likely to score – which in turn is why it helps to know in advance what 'relations' the tester is likely to ask you to 'educe'.

A VOYAGE ROUND THE INTELLECT

Psychologists have constructed various models of intelligence to help them construct tests that they hope will provide some good overall measure that reasonably summarizes it.

But intelligence has many different features, and an IQ score must remain only a shorthand summary number that may be helpful, but is not an exhaustive description of it. The internal volume of a Cadillac's passenger compartment is a useful bit of information for example, and that is why it appears in the sales brochures. But until you know the exact width, height and length of it, you cannot say with certainty whether Aunt Gladys and her skiing equipment will both fit in.

Picturing intelligence, like volume, as the product of several different dimensions has proved quite useful conceptually. But it makes you realize just how complicated the concept might be.

J. P. Guildford, for example, proposed a three-dimensional model of the intellect. Under the first dimension, mental **operations**, he thought that people might have different abilities in terms of cognition, memory, creativity, reasoning and evaluation of the results. Then the **products** of this work could be listed as units, classes, relations, systems, transformations, and implications. The **content** of the tasks could be figural, symbolic, semantic, or behavioural.

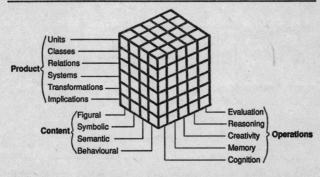

Guildford's model of the intellect

And so on. The trouble is that when you add all that lot up you have 5 x 6 x 4 (= 120) different combinations for a person's performance on a test of all these different abilities. You might be brilliant at some combinations, lousy at others, while someone else might have just the opposite skills. Is it really fair to summarize your different talents in a single IQ figure? And can we really design a simple IQ test that will do justice to all those different combinations?

Eysenck has also pictured intelligence as having three dimensions. All these models are quite arbitrary and the factors you include in your list are a matter of personal judgement. But

Eysenck's model focuses much more specifically on test performance than some more abstract ideas of intelligence. On one side are the differences in people's abilities with various sorts of **test material** – verbal, numerical, and visuo-spatial questions, for example. And whatever sort of question it might be, different combinations of perception, memory, and reasoning are likely to be involved – the **mental processes** making up the second dimension. Test success with all of those combinations will depend in turn on the third dimension, reflecting the **quality** of performance – mental speed, checking for errors, and perseverance.

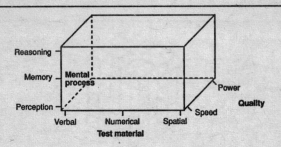

Eysenck's model of intellect

Between them, these elements still provide plenty of material for the intending IQ booster to focus on. Getting better at any one of them means an improvement in your test score, just as the stretched version of the Cadillac will give you more space round Aunt Gladys as well as enough length for her skis.

CHAPTER SIX

WHERE EXACTLY DO YOU STAND?

Even though by this time we have established that raw IQ scores are pretty feeble measures of anything very interesting, the scores which do emerge from different population groups are the stuff of fascination and furore. When Richard Lynn reported the noticeable difference in IQ scores between people in different parts of the British Isles, for example, the *Daily Mirror* headline was 'Irish thicker than English, says a Prof'.

The fascination of these sorts of comparisons is that they make people wonder *why* the differences should occur. Is it the inescapable inheritance of genetics, or the fortune of family, schooling, and environment? Richard Lynn, for example, thought the above-average IQ scores in London and the South-East of England (102.1) owed much to the selective migration of bright people from Scotland and Ireland. The Irish average, a rather poor 96, was also depressed by the rule that priests (who were expected to be literate and therefore tended to be chosen from among the brightest) were supposed to be celibate. Quite whether this is in tune with reality must remain speculative.

LOOKING AT THE DISTRIBUTION

Roughly speaking, when you give a large and representative group of people an IQ test, you find that roughly half score above 100 and half score below. It is not exact because some people have physical handicaps which affect their reasoning ability too, and so the number of people with severe retardation is increased beyond what you might expect. Otherwise, plotting IQ scores against the number of people obtaining them produces a bell-shaped curve, with the bulk of people achieving scores round the 100 mark. Again, it isn't exactly 100 but a little bit over, because the important thing about a good IQ test is that it agrees with everyone else's, not that it divides the population neatly at 100.

How spread out is the bell-shaped distribution? Statisticians say that the standard distribution is about 15. That means that roughly half the population is found in the range of scores from 90 to 110. The bell tapers off quickly until only 2 per cent of the population are found at the MENSA level of 130-something. (Getting any sort of tests to agree when you are dealing with such small samples of people is a miracle that makes you wonder what you're doing wrong rather than how you were so lucky.)

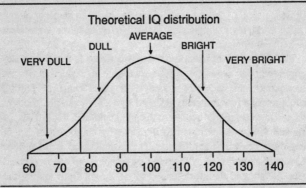

Theoretical IQ distribution

Interestingly, the distribution of scores tends to look very different depending on whether you are using a traditional or a culture-free sort of test. With the traditional test, people tend to be bunched near the centre, but with a culture-free test they are more spread out, producing a much flatter bell-shaped curve.

WHAT IT DOESN'T MEAN

This IQ distribution looks very scientific but we must be careful how we interpret the numbers it summarizes.

For example, one thing we can be sure about is that, with an IQ of 120, you are not twice as clever as a person with an IQ of 60. The scale is quite arbitrary and, although the numbers allow us to place people at various points along it, we cannot perform that kind of mathematical operation on the figures.

Of course we must acknowledge that there is much more to life than IQ. Personal charm, application, persistence, ability to concentrate on a problem – all of these affect how people get on in life (and even their ability to solve reasoning tasks), along with their IQ. There is a broad correlation between IQ and what most people take to be success in life, but even in MENSA one finds people from very different walks of life with a wide spread of achievement among them.

BROKEN DOWN BY AGE AND SEX

Then there is the bad news for anyone intending to grow up. Older people tend to be more spread out than younger ones but, although their knowledge undoubtedly increases over the years, their average IQ score fades steadily. The peak is on average about age 23, which means that the majority of people reading this are over the intelligence hump already. Sorry.

Of course, it is not all bad, because people continue learning as they grow older and know more and more as they progress through life. So you can count yourself wiser, if not more intelligent.

Then there are differences if we compare the scores of all the women in our sample with all the men. Women tend to cluster a bit more about the average. There are fewer up at the genius level, but fewer at the bottom as well. Perhaps it is just nature experimenting with things: you can take more chances with men, who are expendable, but you need more dependability in the constitution of those who are actually left to rear the children.

More difficult to explain is that men tend to do better on visuospatial questions, while women tend to do better on verbal reasoning. That may be one reason why so many women are found in publishing and broadcasting, where verbal skills are at a premium, while architects and chess players tend to be men.

VOCATION AND INTELLIGENCE

Which brings us to the issue of vocation and IQ.

Be mindful of the qualifications that have already been made when looking at the relationship between IQ and vocation. Still, it is at least interesting that different professional groups do demonstrate different average IQ scores. University professors have averages in the 130s, journalists in the mid-120s, mechanics in the mid-100s, barbers around 95, and truck-drivers less than 90.

The link between intelligence and occupation has long been recognized. Gottfried Reinhardt once said that 'there are three kinds of intelligence – the intelligence of man, the intelligence of the animal, and the intelligence of the military – in that order'.

More scientific surveys, however, show that people in the posh jobs do not usually have IQ scores that are far from their professional average, while those doing manual labour exhibit quite a range of IQ. It could be that very dull people can just never learn the intricacies of accountancy, while even a genius can become a lumberjack. Or it may be that the top professions screen themselves from dull applicants by giving them IQ tests. Whatever the reason, it remains a good bet that the brightest truck-driver is a lot sharper than the dullest economics professor – and probably knows a good deal more about making money to boot.

DIFFERENT RACES AND CULTURES

Then there is the argument about the average IQ scores achieved by different racial groups. Since the time of the US Army's widespread use of IQ tests in the First World War, it has been known that American blacks score, on average, about 15 points below the average for American whites. And that, as you might expect, has caused some *real* arguments.

The debate is not so much about the fact that average scores differ but over what the significance of this may be. Remember, for example, that a 15 point IQ difference does not mean that one group is on average 15 per cent less bright than another. And these are mere averages anyway. There is plenty of scatter among the scores of each population and what is important is the performance of the *individual*.

Racial discrimination, leading to a deprived family environment, poor education, instilling lower expectations and producing lower socio-economic status, has been proposed as an explanation for this particular and remarkable difference. And you cannot really correct this by choosing only people from the two groups who happen to have much the same background and economic positions. If they have reached that point it may be because they and their parents were more able than others of the group discriminated against, thereby giving a very skewed sample to work on. The conclusion is that only when the two populations attain equal standing can we really compare their IQ scores.

That argument does not always work, however, because other minority groups suffering racial discrimination and poor living conditions (such as European Jews before the Second World War) sometimes score *higher* than the host population. And Mexican-Americans are, on average, even poorer off in socio-economic terms than American blacks, although they tend to do better on IQ tests. Eskimos do pretty well too (but, of course, most of the Eskimos who have been given IQ tests at all are to be found in the smarter Canadian schools, so again the sampling problem dominates the debate).

It could be that IQ tests are designed by educated whites *for* educated whites. A test which is standardized on such a population could be quite inappropriate for other cultural groups. Some psychologists believe they have found that non-white candidates often score badly because they distrust the testers.

History and politics cloud the discussion. But on the other side, Eysenck concludes that the evidence from tests of different kinds, designed and administered by people of different race and from different countries, suggests very strongly that the results are unaffected by any such factors. Of course, it is always possible to devise culture-bound tests that only the target group can do because their questions centre around group slang, some special range of interests shared by the group, group history, and so forth. But that would be recognized as containing its own bias and could not be standardized usefully against a large population.

NATURE OR NURTURE?

Many scientists have come to the conclusion that genetic factors have much to do with IQ test performance. Some, in the nineteenth century, charged with Darwinian enthusiasm, thought that inheritance might be *all* of the difference, but no detached scholars have seriously maintained that for half a century or more. After collecting and reviewing the evidence Eysenck concludes that heredity is about twice as important as environment in shaping IQ scores.

Eysenck's findings are sometimes taken to imply that heredity is four times as important, which has made him the target of fierce and sometimes physical argument. But that view is a confusion of statistics that he corrects in *Intelligence: Battle for the Mind.*

Whatever the facts of the matter, it is clear that there is a good deal of spread among the IQ scores of any group and that it would be quite wrong to discriminate for or against any group as a whole on the basis of any such average. Properly understood, IQ tests should actually help to break down our prejudices. For example, the common prejudice that people in working-class occupations are stupid, maintained in argument and reinforced by discrimination right to the end of the nineteenth century, has been disproved by scientific testing and certainly could not be adhered to today.

CHAPTER SEVEN

GENERAL RULES TO BOOST YOUR IQ

More people today have experience of IQ tests than before and the debate about intelligence spreads right down into the popular press, therefore people know more about the merits and the deficiencies of the tests themselves.

That, of course, should help to break down some prejudices that the early development and use of IQ tests built up. We should by now recognize that intelligence is not everything a person needs to negotiate life and work successfully. C. Northcote Parkinson saw the point many years ago:

'The defect in the intelligence test is that high marks are gained by those who subsequently prove to be practically illiterate. So much time has been spent in studying the art of being tested that the candidate rarely has time for anything else.'
(*Parkinson's Law or the Pursuit of Progress*, John Murray (Publishers) Ltd.)

Which brings us to the next point: negotiating the art of being tested.

GETTING BETTER

The first rule for boosting your IQ is to do some IQ tests.

People tend to get better scores when they are familiar with the sort of material that IQ testers employ. The greatest improvement comes in the first two or three attempts, and then it tails off. So doing somewhere around three to five tests before the crunch test is effort well spent.

One investigation of test scores in South Africa suggested that with coaching it was possible to raise the scores of European candidates by 10.5 points on average, and the scores of African candidates a whopping 14.5 points. Part of the reason for this potential is that test questions are intended to be novel, testing your reasoning rather than your knowledge. Folk who have never seen anything like them before find themselves at a plain disadvantage. But in fact you can make yourself familiar with their style and so claw back some of that disadvantage.

Indeed, this improvement gained as a result of familiarity is so well known that very serious testers will give candidates several tests before the crucial one just to even out any prior differences in test experience.

The second rule, already mentioned, is to select the sort of test you are good at if at all possible.

From your practice sessions you will quickly learn which sort of questions you prefer – numerical, verbal, or visuo-spatial. If you can sound authoritative in specifying the sort of test you think people ought to be using, they will often give you one that has more of your favourite types of question in it.

The next rule is to be rested, refreshed, and relaxed.

Everybody performs better in examinations when their mind is clear; and when the examination is intended to distinguish speed and accuracy of mental reasoning, the importance of this factor is even greater. Fatigue is no friend of IQ boosters.

A 1989 survey of American businessmen claimed that they often made mistakes and were a bit slow in conducting their deals because they wore their neckties too tight. Fashionable though this might be, it cuts off some of the blood supply to the brain and doesn't do much for anyone's reasoning performance. There must be a lesson for test candidates somewhere in that finding.

Of course, you can resort to artificial stimulants of one kind or another, as some people do when facing examinations. The general habit is probably unwise, of course, and the specific intention may not be served by the use of drugs. There is perhaps too little evidence to judge the exact relationship between drug use and IQ scores since surprisingly little scientific work has been done. But with persistence and accuracy being as important as speed, stimulants may not serve candidates all that well.

The last rule is to go beyond the step of gaining test experience and to make a concerted effort to know the sorts of relation which IQ testers tend to use in designing tests.

Hopefully, the remaining sections of this book should help you to do just that.

PART TWO

ESTIMATING YOUR IQ

CHAPTER EIGHT

SELF-TESTING YOUR IQ

THE BEST POLICY

If you write to MENSA, the high-IQ society, they will send you an intelligence test that you can do at home. Hence the old joke that people seeking to join MENSA want their heads examined.

If you are encouraged by your results and want to go on for membership, the society will arrange to have you professionally assessed under proper test conditions. And if your score on that second test is good enough, you're in.

Even before the days of number-crunching computers, however, it was a well-known fact around the MENSA offices that candidates tend to do much better on the first test than on the second. Not always, by any means – some do worse, which is why it is worth going on to the professional test even if you just miss the qualifying score on the first. But, on average, people score better at home.

That might surprise people who design IQ tests because it is normally expected that people *improve* from one test to the next as they become more familiar with the material and with what is expected of them. The psychologist might conclude that people simply feel more relaxed and comfortable at home and so score better than they do after having travelled to some unfamiliar test centre.

Working mothers, bartenders and others familiar with human nature have a better explanation – people cheat. It is very easy to have a 'quick' look at the questions before you sit down to do the test, or to give yourself an extra minute 'by accident', or even deliberately to 'compensate' for time lost when you dropped your pencil.

Human nature might not be on your side, then, but do try to complete the test that follows as honestly as you can. No peeking at the questions or the answers and no 'compensatory' or 'accidental' extra seconds on the clock. A single IQ test is a pretty poor

measure of anything anyway, but it will only have any meaning at
all if you approach it correctly.

CULTIVATE A HEALTHY DISRESPECT

Estimating your IQ at home on the basis of one self-administered
test is probably about as good as judging your own piano-playing
ability from one chorus of *Für Elise*. Professional psychologists
and musicians would demand something quite different and would
undoubtedly end up with quite a different judgement about your
performance. So treat the test as fun, do the best you can, but do not
get elated or downcast at the result.

Have a healthy disrespect for the result in any case. Your IQ
score is only a single number which cannot possibly encapsulate
all the different strengths and weaknesses people have in solving
various verbal or numerical questions, ones requiring different
degrees of memory and reasoning and so on.

PERFORMANCE ON OTHER TESTS

Remember also that everyone has good days and bad days and in
IQ tests these are probably rather important factors. Only by doing
a number of different tests over the course of a few days would you
really get a secure idea of your IQ through self-testing at home. But
tests do vary.

Every new test has to be tried out on a large number of people
who have done other IQ tests so that the results they give can be
matched up and the new test scores 'standardized' against the old
ones. The trouble is that it is hard to get willing candidates from
those who find IQ tests intimidating or who feel that they have
done badly on IQ tests in the past. People who have passed the
MENSA test and who like doing intelligence puzzles volunteer
thick and fast. Let's face it, though, they are a pretty unusual bunch
and not the most representative group of people on whom to try out
a test that ought to cover a wide range of abilities. So you have to
aim to try out any new test on a mix of different people.

The test which follows, and the one at the back of the book,
have been tried out on different groups to the extent that they are

fine for amusement purposes. But they are not standardized widely enough for accurate professional use. So again, treat them as fun and do not read too much into the result.

BEGINNING THE TEST

To do the test properly you need a good clock or watch so that it will be easy to time yourself precisely. An extra minute here or there can make quite a difference to your score, so it is worth looking out an accurate clock or watch, preferably one with a second hand or a digital second counter.

The best thing is to get somebody else to time you. They will be less tempted to give you more time than you should have (sometimes wickedly so), and their eye on the clock will save you from having to check it all the while and running overtime by mistake.

However, make sure that you are not getting help from anyone else. It is better if other people cannot see the answers you are writing down because even their silent facial expressions can provide hints or prompt you to change an answer that you would otherwise be perfectly happy with.

The answers to all the questions in the test are simple numbers, words, or letters. You don't have to draw anything or spell any complicated words.

You can write your answers down on the test surface or on a separate sheet of paper if you do not want to mark the book. If you are doing that, it may help you to write the numbers 1–60 down the side of the paper so that you can put your answers conveniently alongside without getting mixed up.

The questions test your reasoning ability. There are no sneaky questions that are designed to fool you, although some are more difficult than others.

You have forty-five minutes for the test, which contains sixty items.

Do all the questions before turning to the answers at the back of the book. The answers can be found on page 155.

When you are comfortable and prepared, check your starting time and begin.

CHAPTER NINE

TEST ONE

You have 45 minutes to complete this test

1   Which four-letter word means nearly the same as the words outside the box?

B L A Z E ⎢_ _ _ _⎥ S H O O T

2   Which one of the five given figures could come next?

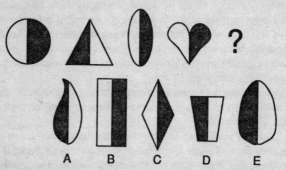

3   What word can be prefixed by any of the letters on the left?

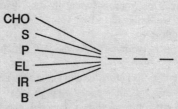

4 Insert the missing number.

10	5	6
16	13	4
?	3	3

5 What word completes the first word and starts the second?

ADO __ __ TRAY

6 Which figure comes next?

7 Insert the missing number.

8   What word completes the first word and starts the second?

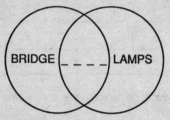

BRIDGE _ _ _ _ LAMPS

9   Which figure comes next?

?

A   B   C   D   E   F

10 Which is the odd one out?

TRENCH   UNDER   OVER   CLOUD   RAIN   GREAT   TOP

11 Insert the missing word.

CLEAT > TOME < STORM
TOTAL > _ _ _ _ < GRASS

12 Which letter comes next?

A Z D W G ?

13 Which figure fits in the space?

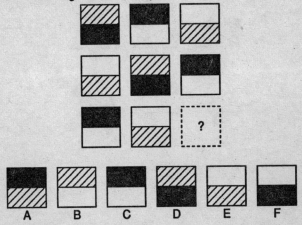

14 Which are the odd two out?

INCH	ARM
FOOT	TAPE
YARD	STONE
CHAIN	TABLE
FURLONG	STEP
MILE	MAIL
LEAGUE	RATE

15   What is the missing number?

$$
\begin{array}{ccc}
6 & 18 & 8 \\
17 & ? & 13 \\
9 & 12 & 11
\end{array}
$$

16   What is the missing word?

GROPE   SLIME   MISER

ASKED   AVERT   _ _ _ _ _

17   Which of the four given figures comes next?

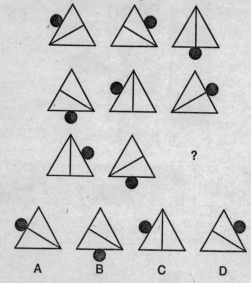

A   B   C   D

18   Insert the missing number.

PARTRIDGE   =   382724516
PEARS   =   36829
TRIPE   =   ?

19 What is the missing number?

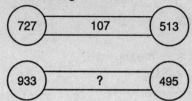

20 What is the missing letter?

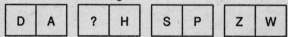

| D | A | ? | H | | S | P | | Z | W |

21 What is the missing number?

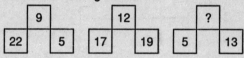

22 Which is the odd one out?

DROW
PHARGRAPA
ENCENTES
LYSET
ESCLAU

23 What are the missing letters?

24 Which letter comes next?

C	J	P	U	?

25 What is the missing word?

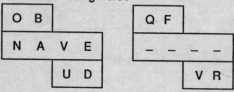

26 Insert the missing number.

1	2	3	4	5
2	9	28	65	?

27 What word completes the first word and starts the second?

C O C K _ _ _ _ _ P I N

28 Which figure completes the relationship?

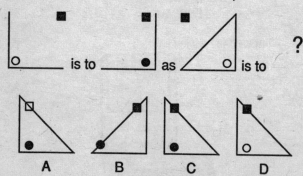

29   What word means nearly the same as each of the given words?

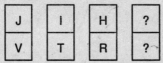

| R U N G | – – – – – | T A L K E D |

30   What is the next domino in the series?

J	I	H	?
V	T	R	?

31   Which figure completes the pattern?

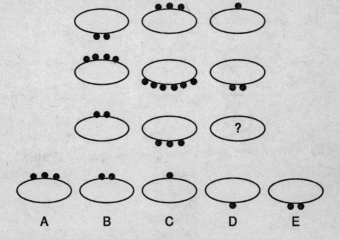

A   B   C   D   E

32   Identify the missing numbers.

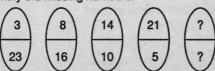

3	8	14	21	?
23	16	10	5	?

33 Which figure completes the picture?

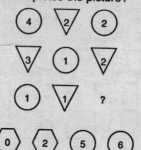

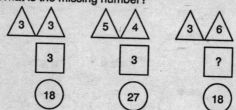

34 What is the missing number?

35 Which word means most nearly the same as LITHE?

AGILE
ABLE
QUICK
ATHLETIC
SUPPLE

36 What is the missing number?

37 What should replace the question-mark?

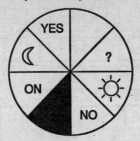

38 Which is the odd one out?

USATARI
KRAMDEN
SNOSOKS
MANGERY

39 What number is missing?

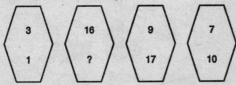

40 Which letter is next?

J   F   M
A   M   J
J   A   S
O   N   ?

41 Identify the missing number.

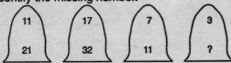

42 Which set of letters comes next?

A	F	G
B	E	I
C	D	H

B	D	H
C	F	G
A	E	I

| C | E | I |
| A | D | H |
| ? |

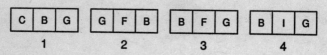

| C | B | G |
| **1** |

| G | F | B |
| **2** |

| B | F | G |
| **3** |

| B | I | G |
| **4** |

43 What number goes in the box?

| 8 3 2 | 2 0 | 1 4 2 |

| 7 0 4 | ? | 2 3 2 |

44 Which figure comes next?

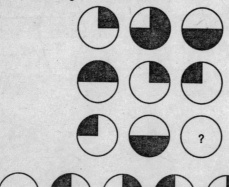

A   B   C   D   E   F

45 Which word belongs in the box?

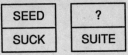

SEED	?
SUCK	SUITE

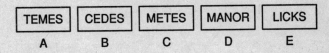

TEMES	CEDES	METES	MANOR	LICKS
A	B	C	D	E

46 What is the missing letter?

BOOK	WAY
NUT	WORM
ARCH	CASE
SUIT	CRACKER
PAT	BISHOP

47 Which numbers belong in the last domino?

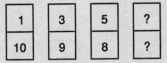

1	3	5	?
10	9	8	?

48 Insert the missing word.

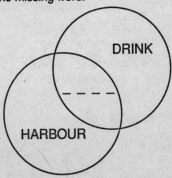

DRINK

- - - -

HARBOUR

49 Identify the missing letters.

50 Identify the odd one out.

ABOVE   EFFECT   GHOUL   LOWER   NOSEGAY   TURN

51 What are the missing numbers?

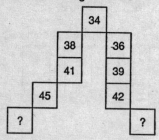

52 Which figure completes the series?

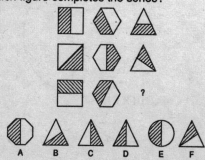

53 What goes in the first domino?

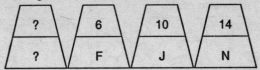

54 Which word is most nearly the opposite of DISAGREE?

MATCH   SETTLE   CONCUR   CONSENT   ACCEDE

55 What is the missing letter?

H	K	F	M	D	O	_

56 What number comes next?

9   5   8   4   7   3   _

57 Which is the odd duck out?

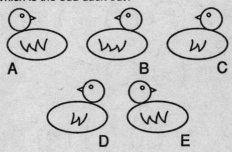

58 What is the missing word?

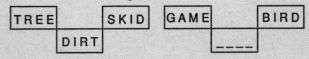

59 Here are four views of the same cube. Which face is the missing one?

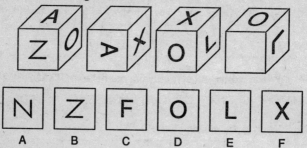

60 Which figure completes the pattern?

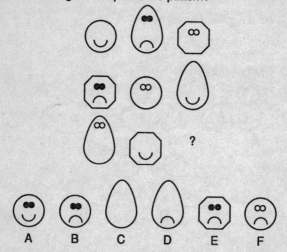

PART THREE

EXERCISES
AND
EXPLANATIONS

CHAPTER TEN

NUMBER QUESTIONS

SERIES QUESTIONS

If you see a string of numbers across the page with a question-mark or a blank space at the end of it, you can be pretty sure you have come across a sequence question, usually called a *series*.

Normally, this means that there is some relationship between each number and the next one in the string. You have to work out the relation and apply that to the last number in order to work out the next number in the series. Take Q1 for example:

Q1: What is the next number in the series?

2 4 6 8 ?

This is an easy one. If you look at the series, you see that it increases steadily. If you look closer, you see that each number in the series is arrived at by adding 2 to the previous number. Add 2 to the last number and you get 10, the missing answer.

Three-pronged attack

Now see what you have done to arrive at this answer. Because although the question is so simple that you probably imagined you got the answer without even thinking, in fact you have gone through three very important steps which are the key to answering all IQ test questions.

It's the old Spearman three-stage process once again. ('What's this?' cry all those who skipped the opening chapters of the book. Well, you don't deserve it, but let's go through it one more time. See page 22.)

Spearman called his three stages:

- the *apprehension* of experience
- the eduction of *relations*; and
- the eduction of *correlates*.

Now in plain English (who on earth goes round educing things?), this means that you are going through the following three steps.

First, you are noticing that something is going on. You notice that the numbers in the sequence are rising, and rising gradually, from left to right. There seems to be some sort of theme linking them.

Second, you *work out the relation*, the theme, that links the individual numbers in the series. In this case, by the application of superlative brainpower, you work out that you have to add 2 to each number to get the next.

Third, you *apply that relation* which you have detected to *work out the next item in the series*. You ask yourself 'If I have to add 2 each time, what do I get when I add 2 to 8?' It's not exactly a very difficult sum.

Different forms of series

Series questions usually have a blank at the end for you to fill in.

Some testers are sneaky, though, and will put the blank at the beginning so that you have to work out the relation and then work backwards – this sort of style:

Q2: Fill in the missing number.

___ 8 11 15 20

In this question, the difference (or as they say in the trade, the 'interval') between the numbers grows by one each time – 3, 4, and 5. That is the relation nicely 'educed'. Then you have to work backwards to see what would be the *first* number in that growing series of intervals – it is 2, of course – and apply that to the first printed term, the 8, to solve the question. The answer is 6, since 8 − 2 = 6 (or, if you like, 6 + 2 = 8).

Another, even sneakier, form is when the blanks appear in the middle of a sequence. Take this question, for example:

Q3: What is the missing number?

5   7   ?   17   25

These can be quite difficult, because more than one step is needed
to work out the relation in the first place. In this question, the series
seems to be increasing fairly steadily, so the first thing we might
look at is the difference. The difference between the first two terms
of the series (5 and 7) is 2, while the difference between the last
two (17 and 25) is 8. And we notice that the gap between the middle ones (7 and 17) is 10.

Well, that gap of 10 is really two differences, so it might be
made up by various combinations: 0 and 10, 1 and 9, 2 and 8, 3 and
7, 4 and 6, or 5 and 5. Now the combination 4 and 6 is an interesting one, because that would give us a neat series of intervals, 2, 4,
6, 8. Add that 4 to the 7 and you get the answer of 11; and if you like
you can add the other 6 and confirm your answer by getting the 17.

Double sequences

Sometimes there is more than one sequence running through a
string of numbers. Often there are two of them mixed up. Try this
one:

Q4: What are the missing numbers?

5   6   7   8   10   11   14   ?   ?

It looks hard until you realize that it is not a single sequence, but
two, going alternately – one of 5, 7, 10, 14 (and then 19, because
the intervals increase by 1 each time) – and one of 6, 8, 11 (and
then 15, because the intervals again grow by 1 each time).

Giveaways: There are several dead giveaways that a particular
series of numbers is in fact two sequences running together, so it is
worth looking out for them, especially if a straightforward
approach looks a bit wobbly.

The first is where you see two blanks to fill in instead of the
usual one. The IQ tester is getting you to give the next term in each
sequence.

The next is where you look at alternate terms and they seem to fit some sort of pattern. Double-sequence questions usually leap-frog in this way, and it is rare to find other ways of constructing them.

Another dead giveaway is where you look at the alternates and you see some numbers going up and others going down:

Q5: What are the missing numbers?

$$5 \quad ? \quad 7 \quad 11 \quad 10 \quad 8 \quad 14 \quad 6 \quad ?$$

Here they are the same sequences as those above, but one goes left to right and the other goes right to left.

The last dead giveaway is the length of the string of numbers. A good IQ tester rarely needs more than four numbers and one blank in a straightforward series question. If you see strings of seven or eight numbers, you know something fishy is going on.

What sort of relations?

There are several common patterns in the numerical sequence question, so it is worth trying them first.

Even Intervals: Even gaps between each term in the series are very easy to spot, which of course makes them rare as IQ test items. However, *falling* sequences with equal intervals are some-times found because they are reckoned to be a mite harder:

Q6: Fill in the missing number.

$$21 \quad 17 \quad 13 \quad 9 \quad ?$$

Here the difference is simply 4, which you subtract from each term to get the next, with 5 being the final answer.

Increasing and decreasing intervals: We have seen examples of increasing gaps of 2, 3, 4 and so on. Decreasing intervals such as 5, 4, 3, 2 are also fairly standard.

Perhaps more common are intervals that increase by regularly rising amounts, such as this example:

Q7: Insert the missing number.

1   5   13   25   ?

The intervals here (4, 18, 12) rise by 4 each time, so the next should be 16, giving 41 (25 + 16) as the final answer.

Adding terms: A widespread series question involves adding each pair of terms to get the next one. Thus:

Q8: What is next in the series?

1   2   3   5   8   ___

is a very common question, giving the answer 13 (= 5 + 8). And no doubt you can imagine more elaborate versions of the same principle.

Multiplication: All the sequences we have dealt with so far have risen fairly gently. That is a good sign that it is some sort of adding or subtracting relationship that you must look for. When a sequence rises or falls very fast, however, you should begin to suspect something else. For instance:

Q9: What is the next number in the series?

2   6   18   54   ?

This series rises at such a rate that you should begin looking for some sort of multiplication link. Try any pair of the sequence terms and you see that you have to multiply each number by 3 to get the next. So 54 x 3 gives 162, which is the answer.

The number you have to keep multiplying by to make a series work – 3 in this question – is not normally very great, otherwise the arithmetic gets a bit much.

Squares and cubes: It is very rare indeed to find questions growing by cubes (a number multiplied by itself, and then by itself again) because their rise soon gets alarming, the numbers get into the thousands, and people sitting the test start making arithmetical errors instead of reasoning errors, so the test isn't doing its job.

Squares (where you multiply a number by itself) are used quite a bit, but again there are limits to their deployment. Each term in the following series:

Q10: What is the next number?

$$2 \quad 4 \quad 16 \quad 256 \quad \underline{\quad}$$

is the square of the previous number, and you can work out the last one for yourself. That sort of question gets unmanageable so fast that you never see it.

What you do see, though, are sequences made from the square of some straightforward arithmetical series. Thus:

Q11: Fill in the blank.

$$1 \quad 4 \quad 9 \quad 16 \quad 25 \quad \underline{\quad}$$

The numbers here are simply the squares of 1, 2, 3, 4, 5 (and then 6). That is a common sort of pattern.

If anything, these square questions grow rather less mightily than the multiplication ones. And it is not normal to have squares of a more elaborate sequence involving larger numbers (such as 2, 4, 8, 12, 16) because the arithmetic gets a bit hairy. So look for the simple ones first.

Two-stage formulae: Even questions with squares in do not really take a great deal of fathoming out, so many of the series questions you find in IQ tests involve two different mathematical operations.

So you might have to do a multiplication and then add or subtract some number. The following is an example:

Q12: What is the missing number?

$$6 \quad 11 \quad ? \quad 41 \quad 81$$

A first look shows it's growing fast enough to be a multiplication puzzle, and the numbers are roughly doubling each time. But as well as *doubling* them, we must *subtract* 1 each time. Thus 11 x 2 gives us 22; subtract 1 and that gives the answer 21. Check it by doubling (to 42) and subtract 1 . . . yes, that is on target.

Sometimes it is a series of squares, plus or minus some number. Such as:

Q13: What is the next term in the series?

$$1 \quad 2 \quad 5 \quad 10 \quad 17 \quad ?$$

This is just a set of the squares of 0, 1, 2, 3, 4 (and 5) with 1 added to each. Thus the answer 26 is arrived at by squaring 5 (5 x 5 = 25) and adding 1.

COPIED RELATIONSHIPS

Another form of the numerical question is where there is one example of a mathematical relationship which you have to translate on to another set of figures.

Take the following example, which is quite common in form:

Q14: Insert the missing number.

$$185 \quad (141) \quad 97$$
$$89 \quad (\quad) \quad 103$$

The answer here is found by adding the numbers outside the brackets and halving the result. So 89 + 103 gives you 192, halve that to get 96, and you have solved the question.

Such questions are really just the numerical form of the common sort of IQ question '__ is to __ as __ is to __'. You know the sort of thing:

Q15: What is the missing colour?

Tomato is to *red* as *pea* is to _____.

Not very hard. The relation is that the first term is a food, and the second is its colour. Peas, of course, are *green*. (Don't bother writing in with objections based on the fact that tomatoes are often green as well, or that yellow tomatoes are now quite fashionable. The question is only for illustration.)

Now, in a series question, the prevailing relationship between each item is repeated a few times. You discover the relation, then apply it to find the next term in the sequence. In questions of the copied relationship however, there is only one opportunity to find the relationship. You might think that would make it harder, but there are a couple of things working in your favour.

First, the form of the question can usually give you a hint. In the case above, you know from the look of the question that it is not a sequence. Instead, you have to do something to the outside numbers to get the inside one, as the layout of the question strongly suggests.

Second, the numbers are usually pretty large, and by eyeing them up you can make a rough guess about what is going on before you move towards working out your solution. The numbers have to be large because there cannot be any ambiguity if you are only getting one example of the relationship. So an opening line of the sort:

$$2 \quad (4) \quad 6$$

would leave you perplexed. Is the middle number half-way between the outside one, half the sum of the outside ones, the difference between the outside ones, the sum of the outside ones minus 4, or what? Each rule would give you a different answer when applied to another row of figures, so the question would be useless.

Generally, when faced with questions using this layout of numbers outside the brackets, you can expect four common possibilities:

● add the outer numbers (or find the difference between them); and
● multiply the result (or divide it) by some number to get the inner number.

So you will see solutions such as:

● add the outer ones and multiply by 3;
● add the outer ones and divide by 10;
● halve the difference between the outers; or

● double the difference between the outers.

Other forms

Designs: Sometimes the question is the same, but the numbers are fitted into a design of some sort. It could be a box:

Q16: Insert the missing number.

25	27	83

86	?	70

Which in this case gives the answer of 39, derived from taking a quarter of the sum of the outer numbers. Or it may be some more elaborate figure:

Q17: What is the missing number?

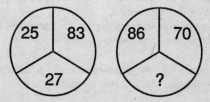

Or one such as:

Q18: Complete the figure.

9	3	17	21
	12	20	?

Here the lower numbers are simply the sum of the two numbers above them.

Again, it is a fairly good bet that the type of diagram used will give you a hint about how to reach the answer – so do think what it is that the question designer is trying to tell you.

Misplaced blank: You might even find that the blank is not in the usual place. Thus:

Q19: Insert the missing number.

$$185 \quad (141) \quad 97$$
$$89 \quad (96) \quad ?$$

Which is just a different form of a question that we have seen before (Q14).

ARITHMETICAL OPERATIONS

You can be called upon to do mathematical operations of various kinds. They might be more elaborate than the straightforward translation of one relationship into another set of figures, or require an extra step or two of reasoning.

Nevertheless, in questions of this kind, looking at the *form* of the question, the way it is laid out, in order to get some clue about how to solve it, is a useful trick.

The shape of a question can suggest the mathematical operation you have to go through to get the answer.

Magic squares: Take the grid format known as the magic square. It is a very common sort of IQ test question, like so:

Q20: Insert the missing number.

$$
\begin{array}{ccc}
5 & 17 & 7 \\
16 & ? & 12 \\
8 & 11 & 10
\end{array}
$$

In the magic square, all the rows and all the columns add to the same number, in this case 29, giving 1 as the missing answer.

Shapes: Sometimes different shapes indicate the different operations you must go through to reach the correct result, as in:

Q21: Fill in the missing number.

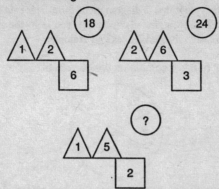

Adding the numbers in the triangles and multiplying by the one in the square gives you the answer in the circle, 12. Or again:

Q22: What number completes the figure?

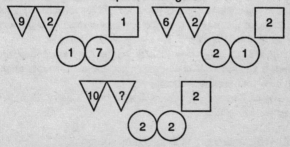

In this item the difference of the numbers in triangles, divided by the product of the numbers in circles, equals the number in the square, so 2 is the answer (you could make a reasonable case for 18 as well).

FIGURES, FAMILIAR AND EXOTIC

Circles, squares, boxes and all the other paraphernalia can help you get to the right answers. But others are just there to confuse.

Disguised sequences: It is quite common to have a straightforward series question presented in diagrammatic form. This is intended to throw you off the scent, but of course now you know the trick, you won't be so easily diverted. To take an example:

Q23: What number completes the cartwheel?

That is the question which appeared on the cover of Hans Eysenck's *Know Your Own IQ*, and the official answer is 33, which you get by doubling the preceding number as you go round and then subtracting 1. (17 x 2 = 34, 34 − 1 = 33). But just to show that even the master can be caught out by ambiguous question design, in the previous example you could reasonably put down 1. If you imagine the blank as coming at the *beginning* of the sequence instead of at the end, you would have 1½ x 2 = 3, 3 − 1 = 2 – which would fit.

Still, it's certainly wiser to settle on the more straightforward answer if you see such an ambiguity, because the examiner might well miss your ingenious alternative.

Another disguised sequence comes from Thierry Carabin's *Testez Votre Logique*:

Q24: Which numbers fit in the blank squares?

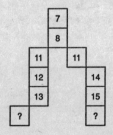

By the layout of this question, the author has conveniently hinted to us that in any column, dropping down a square adds 1; while moving a column left or right adds 2. So the answers are 16 and 16.

Other sequences can be given away like this. For example:

Q25: What is the missing number?

1	2	3	4	5
1	4	9	16	?

The grid makes it look confusing, but really the figures on the bottom row are just the squares of the ones above, giving 25 as the answer.

Double sequences often turn up in dominoes:

Q26: Which numbers fit in the domino?

4	9	15	22	?
1	5	10	16	?

The top sequence has an interval which increases by 1 each time (5, 6, 7, and so 8), while the bottom sequence does the same, starting from an interval of 4. Thus the answer is 30 and 23.

Relation to number opposite: Some diagrams do not work as sequences, but are drawn to suggest some uniform arithmetical relationship between a number and another one at some significant point – say opposite, as in:

Q27: Insert the missing number.

The obvious answer to this question would be 12, since a sequence does not fit and the numbers in the bottom half are simply nine times those opposite. You could be perverse and say 972, but don't expect to be credited for it.

Another version is on this style:

Q28: What number is missing?

In this circle, the numbers in the top half must be doubled, and then 1 subtracted, to get the corresponding number in the bottom, so 7 is the answer.

GETTING INTO TRAINING

Now you know all there is to know about the various kinds of mathematical question you are likely to face on an IQ test. So why not get into training by running through the assortment on the following pages?

You will find the answers on page 159.

NUMBERS QUIZ

Instructions:

In each of the questions below, fill in the missing number or numbers indicated by the question-marks.

Q29:   5   12   ?   54   110

Q30:

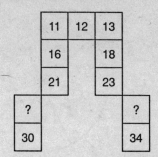

Q31:   10   12   22   24   34   ?

Q32:   3   8   ?   21

Q33:   -1   2   7   14   ?

Q34:

Q35:

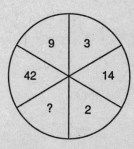

Q36:

9	10	8	11	?
26	25	27	?	28

Q37:

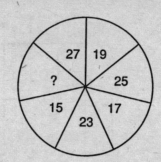

Q38:

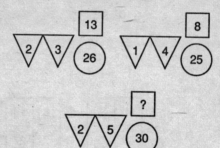

CHAPTER ELEVEN

ALPHABETICAL QUESTIONS

SEQUENCES

Eight times out of ten, you can be sure that when you see apparently unconnected strings of letters in a test question, it is some sort of alphabetical sequence or series.

And, of course, you have learnt most of the trick of doing this sort of question from the coaching on number questions that you have just gone through. The only difference in the alphabetical version is that the series is based on the letter's position in the alphabetical sequence – the familiar A, B, C – instead of the numerical sequence starting with 1, 2, 3.

Take a typical and simple question of this sort:

Q39: What is the missing letter?

B   D   F   H   ?

Getting the answer to this is just a case of skipping alternate letters in the alphabet. You miss out A, C, E, G, I and that leaves you with J as the correct solution.

Sometimes, just like the numerical series questions, the interval between the letters increases or decreases according to some sort of rule. Here is one:

Q40: Which letter is next?

A   E   J   P   ?

The interval in this question increases by one each time, giving W as the answer.

And just as in the numerical questions, the blanks can come at the beginning or the end of a series. Two blanks are again a pretty good indicator of a double sequence at work, though some testers fool you by leaving only one blank to fill in:

Q41: Complete the series.

A   Z   C   X   E   ?

This series in fact contains two sequences. Once again they are alternating letters in the alphabet, but the first goes forward starting from A while the second works backwards from Z, giving V as the missing letter.

Hints on your approach

Usually, it is not a very difficult relationship that links the various letters in the series. There are three reasons for this.

First, you are starting off with the alphabet and then doing some counting, up or down, to find the various positions of the letters involved. In other words you are going through two steps rather than one. To ask you then to perform some complicated mathematical task would be a bit much. It would take you too long and you would make the occasional mistake in the mathematics or the translation of your sequence number back into letters. So the test would not be examining what it was supposed to.

Second, there are only 26 letters in the alphabet, while numbers can go into the hundreds or thousands. So on even moderately difficult IQ questions, with only 26 items to play with, the tester must keep the reasoning rule more simple.

Third, you certainly cannot expect to have square or cubic relationships determining the alphabetical position of one letter against another. These and other multiplication rules are much more appropriate to numbers than to letter positions, and in any case they quickly escalate off the end of the alphabetical sequence.

So most of the rules you will see are additions or subtractions – every third letter, every alternative letter backwards, one letter forward then three back, intervals growing by one or two each time.

Getting a double sequence is about the hardest you are likely to find, so look out for it if the more straightforward rules do not fit.

Another point about alphabetical series is that you normally go round to A again once you have reached Z. An example of this is provided by the following question:

Q42: Which letter is next?

S   V   Y   B   ?

The sequence here is formed by taking every third letter in the alphabet, and taking A to follow directly after Z. Thus B is three along from Y, and the missing letter, E, is three along from that.

You could theoretically go round and round several times, going back to A after you have landed on Z, but by this time things have become very complicated and such questions are rare indeed.

GRAPHIC LAYOUTS

Alphabetical letter questions can be laid out in several different ways. Some of them are intended to suggest, or disguise, sequences, just as in their numerical counterparts. Others are there to suggest different sorts of relationship.

Simple square

A grid of letters normally suggests that something is going on between different rows or between different columns. There may not be anything significant about the particular letters in any individual row or column, but they are linked in some regular way to their counterparts in other rows and columns.

It might be that all the letters in one column are two places further down the alphabet than their counterparts in the first; or that the interval between each letter in a row and the letter immediately below it is the same. An example will show this sort of thing at work:

Q43: Which is the missing letter?

T   Q   M
P   L   G
V   Q   ?

The letters in the second column go back two, three, and four spaces over those in the first; the letters in the third column go back three, four, and five spaces, giving K as the correct answer. A difficult one.

Dominoes

The domino format can disguise a perfectly straightforward sequence, or suggest a repeated relationship, as it does in the question below:

Q44: Insert the missing letter.

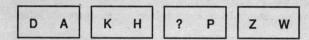

There is an interval of three, going right to left, on each domino, giving S as the answer.

Dominoes also strongly suggest a double series. You might have one series in the top deck of the dominoes and another in the bottom deck, for example. But one of the IQ testers' favourites is this:

Q45: What are the missing letters?

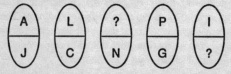

– where the sequences alternate from the top of one to the bottom of the next, then up to the top again. In this particular version, the sequences also alternate through the alphabet, skipping one letter each time, giving E and R as the answer to the question.

Cartwheels

Most IQ testers know better than to put sequence questions in the cartwheel format for the same reason that they avoid them with numbers – depending on which way you go round, you can get two entirely different answers. Take this one:

Q46: Insert the missing letter.

It's a simple enough sequence of alternate letters and, if you go clockwise, you get the answer O. If you go anticlockwise, however, and follow the A follows Z (or in this case the Z follows A) rule, you come up with the answer Y, two back from A.

So usually, you will find that a cartwheel presentation, common enough in IQ tests, is not a sequence. It could be simply a fancy kind of domino question with copied relationships, or doing something that dominoes cannot quite do:

Q47: What letter is missing?

Here, the interval between the letters is symmetrical above and below the horizon, giving H as the answer.

Other forms can suggest the same kind of copied relationship. For instance:

Q48: What letter is missing?

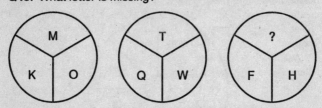

In these circles, the letter at the top is midway between the letters in the lower two, as they appear in the alphabet, giving G as the solution.

When letters become words

Life is not always quite so easy. As well as putting letters into alphabetical strings and playing about with them, you can also form them into words. Some questions that look at first glance to be letter questions turn out to be word questions. For example:

Q49: Insert the missing letters.

It may look like a sequence, and you might find yourself struggling to fit some pattern to it. But in fact it is a word, reading clockwise. This example comes from Eysenck, whose given answer is S and T, making up the word HESITATE. However, R and G would fit equally well, making up the word HERITAGE.

There are some giveaway signs to watch for. Firstly, cartwheel questions are not usually sequences. Second, there tend to be more vowels – A, E, I, O, U – than you would expect in a normal sequence because you need at least one, and often more than one, in almost every word. Third, there are wild swings from one end of the alphabet to the other which does not exactly suggest an orderly sequence.

Another example of the same principle at work comes from Glenn Wilson's engaging compendium of intelligence questions, *Improve Your IQ*:

Q50: What is the missing letter?

It's an amusing question, giving the answer C, which completes the name ENOCH POWELL and the affiliation CONSERVATIVE.

But at the same time, this question does show how IQ test items can occasionally become dated. Not only did Enoch Powell leave the Conservative Party in 1974, but he left Parliament entirely in 1987. Undoubtedly his name, once widely known, will fade in the public's mind as time rolls on.

In another published IQ test, the answer to one question was TAXIMETER-CABRIOLET. Who calls them anything but taxi-cabs nowadays?

Meaning and significance

Usually in questions involving letter series, you do not expect the letters to have some ulterior meaning. Take this specimen:

Q51: Insert the missing letters.

J ? M A M J J ? S O N ?

It looks formidable as a series and, if it were, you might expect to find two or three different sequences going on within it. But in fact it is just the initial letters of the twelve months of the year, starting with January, so F, A and D are the missing ones.

You could have other strings like this, such as the names of playing cards – A K Q J and so on. This one from Philip Carter and Ken Russell goes a bit further:

Q52: Which letter comes next?

M V E M J S U N ?

In that one, you have to know the order of the planets out from the sun, starting from Mercury and going on to Saturn, Uranus, Neptune and – starting with P – Pluto. This question requires a sufficient degree of scientific knowledge that you would be unlikely to find it in a simple IQ test, but it is an amusing one to puzzle on. As is the following question from same authors:

Q53: Should K go above or below the line?

A   E   F   H   I

   B   C   D   G   J

This is one of those questions that makes you kick yourself when you see the answer. It goes above: all the straight letters go above, all the curved ones go below.

That does it for letter questions, but before we go into word questions where it is all about meaning, let's have a quick look at some letter and number combinations, which you see quite a lot in IQ tests.

CHAPTER TWELVE

MIXED NUMBERS AND LETTERS

It is quite common to see questions that use a mixture of letters and numbers and there are some fairly standard patterns to these as well. As you might be expecting by now, we will start with sequences again.

SERIES QUESTIONS

There are two possible reasons why you might find letters and numbers mixed up in what is obviously a series question.

Dual sequences

The first is that it is there to confuse you. There might in fact be two sequences, one with letters and one with numbers, going on at the same time. This would be a typical question, laid out in the familiar domino style:

Q54: Fill in the missing items.

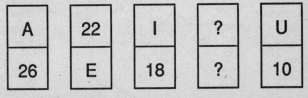

By now you are fluent with this pattern. The letter sequence runs top-bottom-top, and the number sequence runs bottom-top-bottom, and so on. The letters are simply all the vowels in the order they appear in the alphabet, giving O as the missing letter; the numbers descend by 4 each time, giving 14 as the missing number.

Numbers as operators

The other possibility is that the numbers are there not to confuse you but to help you.

Often they signify some procedure or operation that you have to go through to get to the next letter in the series.

Commonly, the numbers tell you how many spaces you have to go forward or back in order to get to the right place in the alphabet. For example:

Q55: Which letter comes next?

B 2 D 6 J 1 K 5 ?

The numbers here are telling you how far you need to advance through the alphabet to reach the next letter. Two spaces down from B you reach D, another 6 down you reach J, and 5 down from K you reach P, the answer.

The movement through the alphabet can be upwards or downwards, and sometimes the shape of the question might change, such as in the following item:

Q56: What is the missing number?

Going clockwise in this question, you add or subtract the appropriate number of letters to reach the next item in the alphabet. Thus six letters on from E is K, three back is H, seven back is A. Four on from A is E, so +4 is the answer.

Translation into letters

Sometimes it can be a numerical sequence that you have to work out first, and then you can translate that number back into the alphabetical sequence. This question shows the principle at work:

Q57: Fill in the missing items.

1   4   9   16   ?

*   *   *   *   *

A   D   I   P   ?

The numerical series is actually a simple enough one, the squares of the first five whole numbers, 1, 2, 3, 4, 5. So on the top deck is the missing number 25. Then you simply go down the alphabet by that number of letters – nine down the alphabet you come to I, sixteen down you come to P, and twenty-five down you come to Y, and that's the missing letter.

CODES

That principle of translating from numbers to a position in the alphabetical sequence is also used in code questions. Here is an example of one of these:

Q58: What is the missing word?

4 5 1 6   18 9 19 5

D E A F   _ _ _ _

The most common rule in all these code questions is that 1 = A, 2 = B, 3 = C, and so on through the alphabet. Following this simple rule allows you to translate the numbers 4, 5, 1, 6 into D E A F, and doing the same with 18, 9, 19, 5 will give you R I S E.

Codes the easy way

If you are doing a test which relies heavily on letter-number questions, you can save yourself some time by jotting down the letters of the alphabet with their numerical place in the queue next to them:

```
 1  2  3  4  5  6  7  8  9 10 11 12 13 14 15 16 17 18 19 20 21 22 23 24 25 26
 |  |  |  |  |  |  |  |  |  |  |  |  |  |  |  |  |  |  |  |  |  |  |  |  |  |
 A  B  C  D  E  F  G  H  I  J  K  L  M  N  O  P  Q  R  S  T  U  V  W  X  Y  Z
```

It doesn't take long to do, and if you are facing two or three questions like this, it is well worth the effort. Often, having the numbers
and letters written down helps you to avoid the simple calculation
mistakes that occur when you are trying to do complex operations
in your head.

Now if you scan the test paper quickly and see only one or two
alphabetical questions, you might not think that it is really worth
doing all this, and you might try to crack the codes in your head.

Well, that's fine if you can do it, but make it easy on yourself.
Do the easy letters first and see if they suggest a word. Then, if
they strongly suggest a particular word, you can check it quite
quickly – much more quickly than by plugging through the alphabet for each letter one at a time.

In the example above, for instance, you might start with the 5,
which if you assume the 1=A, 2=B rule, you quickly discover is
an E. Four along (why start from 1=A again when you are already
on 5=E?) you find I. Between them those strongly suggest the
shape of the word, and in many cases they would limit your
choice to a small number of possibilities. In this one there are
umpteen words of the shape __I__E, as crossword addicts are
well aware, so you have to plug through the alphabet. But even
so, you can see that the first and third letters are consecutive
ones, and if you are prepared for it you can locate the right letters
fairly quickly. Check it, though, because a simple guess at this
stage might give you S I T E, since S and T are in roughly the
right place – but not quite.

Other codes

Sometimes you will be given a word and the numbers (or symbols)
adjacent to the letters give you the clue you need to construct
another word – but it is not a straightforward 1 = A, 2 = B rule. Try
this one:

Q59: What is the missing word?

7 5 6 2 3 1 4 5 1

C O M P A N I O N

8 9 3 0 4 0 * % $

P L A T I T U D E

8 3 1 0 5 6 4 6 $

– – – – – – – – –

Each number or symbol in this question stands for a different letter of the alphabet. Though the order of the link is arbitrary, the same number or symbol always stands for the same letter. Plug in the right letters (8=P, 3=L, $=E etc) and you get PANTOMIME.

Other operations

IQ test designers love things which look like something they are not. Take this pair of sums:

Q60: What completes the sum?

    B O G   B A D

+   –

    2 0 0   2 8 3

    ───────   ───────

    D O G

The trick here is to see that the numbers are simply telling you how many letters to advance in the alphabetical sequence. Two along from B is D, nothing along from O and G is still O and G – so you get D O G. In the right-hand sum, this rule gives you D I G, the correct answer.

Vowels and consonants

Sometimes the question looks like a series of words, but in fact it is the individual letters that are important. And quite commonly in questions of this kind, the vowels (A, E, I, O, U) are given some different numerical weight from the consonants. For instance:

Q61: How heavy is MANGANESE?

Metal	Weight
LEAD	6
COPPER	8
ALUMINIUM	14
GOLD	5
MANGANESE	?

Plainly this has nothing to do with the actual weights of the metals, otherwise gold and lead would have high numbers and aluminium would have a low one. And who knows the relative weights of these things anyway, except metallurgists? No, the answer is found from assigning the value 1 to all the consonants, and 2 to all the vowels, which gives 13 in the case of manganese.

There are other ways in which the numbers can relate to a word rather than strings of letters. Sometimes they are a clue to a word question, or to associations in meaning between different words. Take this one, for example:

Q62: What is the missing number?

BLEEDING	5	HOUSEMAID'S	4
PARSON'S	4	TENNIS	5
LOUD	5	SQUARE	3
DEAF	_	EVIL	3

The words here are the first of a pair that make up well-known phrases — bleeding heart, parson's nose, loud-mouth, evil eye, square leg, tennis elbow, housemaid's knee. The numbers indicate the length of the second word in each pair. In this case, it could only be 'deaf ear', so 3 is the correct number to fill in.

GETTING INTO TRAINING

You are doing well: not only are you now an expert on numerical questions, but you can do questions with letter strings and with combinations of letters and numbers too. Limber up with the questions on the following pages.

You will find the answers on page 159.

LETTERS AND NUMBERS QUIZ

Q63: How far is it to Edinburgh?

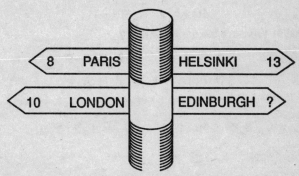

Q64: Which letter comes next in the series?

    J   E   Z   U   _

Q65: Complete the following series:

    S   M   T   W   T   F   ?

Q66: What comes off RUMP to get LOIN?

M I N T	R U M P
+	−
3 6 4 0	_ _ _ _
P O R T	L O I N

Q67: What word fits inside the brackets?

SING　(GIRL)　RULE
GARB　(　　)　CAKE

Q68: Insert the missing number and letter.

1	2	3	5	7	11	13	??
Q	M	K	G	?	C	B	A

Q69: Insert the missing letter.

$$4D + 6J + 7Q - 3N + 11?$$

Q70: What are the missing words?

1 2 3 4 5 6 7 2 8 9

O R C H E S T R A L

3 5 9 9 1 6　　　3 4 1 2 8 9

– – – – – –　　　– – – – – –

Q71: Fill in the missing items.

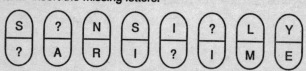

21	19	16	12	7	?
D	F	I	M	R	?

Q72: Insert the missing letters.

S / ? ・ ? / A ・ N / R ・ S / I ・ I / ? ・ ? / I ・ L / M ・ Y / E

CHAPTER THIRTEEN

WORDS, WORDS, WORDS

Word questions pose difficulties for IQ testers.

For a start, they do not translate into other languages. There may be slight differences in nuance or in the familiarity of different words. The familiarity problem is increased because some languages (English, for example) have many more words than others (such as German), so there is more chance of coming across an unfamiliar word.

The translation problem also applies to letter questions, of course. The Western alphabet does not translate into Japanese, Arabic, or Cyrillic characters.

When you try to translate a word question into another language, therefore, you might end up with a translated question that is very much harder or easier than the original. That makes it impossible to use them to compare accurately the IQ scores of different people speaking different languages.

Also, the answers to some word questions can be as much a matter of education as of native intelligence. People who have learnt the proper meaning of words or who have been taught the rules of grammar have a much better chance of scoring well on many questions than those who have not been so fortunate.

Nevertheless, despite these reservations, word questions come up in one guise or another quite often. So let us look at the most common forms.

SYNONYMS AND ANTONYMS

One favourite is to ask you to select a word that is nearest in meaning to the test word. For instance:

Q73: Underline the word which is nearest in meaning to the word DIFFERENT

irregular abnormal unlike strange unusual

In this case, the answer is UNLIKE. Or the question might be phrased so that you are asked to give the meaning which is most nearly the opposite:

Q74: Underline the word which means most nearly the opposite of EXCLUDE

admit, count, register, allow, receive

Here it is the word ADMIT which means most nearly the opposite.

It is rather difficult to give many rules to help you with this sort of question: it is designed to test your appreciation of the nuances of different words and in many cases you either know them or you don't. Nevertheless, there are some things you should be looking for.

All words have a sort of core meaning. They get over one sharp idea. But swirling around that core meaning is a cloud of other ideas that are also conveyed by the word. So the core meaning of the word PROFESSOR is someone who teaches in college, but it also conveys ideas such as absent-minded, boring, crusty, unworldly, scatterbrained, and so on.

In most of these synonym/antonym questions, you have to focus in on the central meaning of the word and then find the match for it. All the other ideas that are attached will take you down the wrong trail. And often, the test designer picks the alternatives so that they do precisely that – unless you are very careful and smell the red herring.

Thus, people do indeed say "Well, it's different" when they mean that something is unusual or unpleasantly strange. But those are just appendages cluttering up the meaning. You have to get to the core meaning: things that are *different* are in fact *unlike*.

WORD COMPLETION

Another common task is when you are told to select the word or the sequence of letters which makes complete new words from a number of different words or prefixes. Such as:

Q75: What is the three-letter word that can be prefixed by all the following?

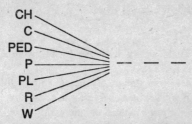

The answer to this one is ANT, which is straightforward enough. Put it together with the given prefixes, and it makes words such as cant, pedant, plant, want, and so on.

When you are doing these questions, remember that the pronunciation of the word-ending you are looking for might be changed by the particular prefix. The pronunciation of the word ANT is universal. But the traditional British pronunciation of CHANT is different from the American. And in PEDANT the A has a different, unstressed, pronunciation yet again. W-prefixes quite often mess up your pronunciation yet again, as WANT testifies.

Clever test designers go to some lengths to find words that you wouldn't think go together because the stress or the pronunciation is altered depending upon the prefix in question. So watch out for those that might change – vowels in particular.

Completing two words

A familiar sort of question is one where you have to discover the word which completes two other words – usually a word which can end one and begin another. Take this specimen:

Q76: What is the word that would complete the first word and begin the second?

UNDER(_ _ _ _ _)WIDE

This one is answered by the word WORLD, which gives you UNDERWORLD and WORLDWIDE. These questions do not necessarily have to deal in whole words, of course:

Q77: What is the word that goes with the suffix and the prefix outside the brackets to form two words?

OB(_ _ _)RAL

OB and RAL are nonsense, just a prefex and a suffix. They are made into whole words, however, by the word LATE, giving OBLATE and LATERAL.

There are various things to watch out for in these questions. Usually, what you are being asked for is a whole word. But it may not be. It may be just a number of letters which would form a complete word with the given prefixes and suffixes.

Usually, the number of letters in the word you are being asked for is indicated by the number of dashes. Normally you will be told this in the instructions to the test, but it is easy to overlook. Dashes are often used instead of question-marks or blanks in numerical or letter questions as well.

Another point to remember is that some of the words you will come up with seem rather obscure. The word OBLATE, for example, is not one which you would normally throw into polite conversation at the breakfast table. Do not let it worry you. The question is designed to investigate the size of the vocabulary you have accumulated over the years, as well as your ability to perform reasoning tasks with those words.

And as in the earlier case, pronunciation changes can play havoc. Take this:

Q78: What word would start the word on the right of the brackets and finish the one on the left?

BE(_ _)ONE

The solution is AT (although there may be other reasonable candidates) – but the pronunciation of that short word changes markedly when it forms BEAT, while the pronunciation of ONE is changed markedly when it is made into ATONE. So again, look for likely combinations of vowels and consonants that could mislead you.

BRIDGES IN MEANING

Some questions look quite similar to those above but what is being sought is not a word that completes others, rather one which means much the same as others.

Usually those other words are completely different in meaning, and the one you are to come up with acts as a sort of bridge between them. Take this question, for example:

Q79: Insert the word which means nearly the same as the words outside the brackets.

DROOP (_ _ _ _) STANDARD

The word FLAG means nearly the same – a standard is a sort of flag, and a drooping flower can be said to flag.

Test designers take special pleasure in examples like this, where the word can be either a noun (a 'thing' word) or a verb (a 'doing' word) according to which one it is matched with.

The word that the tester is looking for does not have to be a completely precise synonym, as it does in synonym questions. Rather, it is the associations of the word, or the various things and actions which it could cover, that you have to match up. Take the specimen:

Q80: Insert the word which means roughly the same as the words outside the box.

TOOL [_ _ _ _ _] TREE

The missing word here is in fact a *type* of tool and a *type* of tree – PLANE.

Or the same with verbs and nouns attempting to confuse you:

Q81: What word means roughly the same as the words outside the brackets?

FIGHT (_ _ _) CONTAINER

The answer BOX suggests itself; though with CONTAINER it is a noun, with FIGHT it becomes a verb. For those who came up with the answer SOCK – good try, but no cigar.

The really nasty ones are where the pronunciation of the word also changes depending on how it is used, but there are precious few of those.

ODD MAN OUT

In odd man out questions, you have to consider a list of items and think about which one does not really fit in.

So you are looking for some link between all the words, and trying to find if one does not fit in with that linkage rule.

There are several sorts of questions like this. For example:

Q82: Underline the odd one out.

walked, rode, sailed, travelled, flew

They are all ways of getting about, so it may seem as if there is no odd man out here. One, however, is different: most are specific ways of going places, whereas TRAVELLED is non-specific. So that is the one you should underline.

This is typical of questions of this sort and your ability to spot it depends upon your appreciation of the meanings and implications of each word in the list. The nature of the difference you are being asked to detect varies from question to question. Sometimes it is a difference in the core meaning of the words. Sometimes it is a quality which all the objects described, bar one, possess – all mammals except OSTRICH, all in the Northern hemisphere except SYDNEY, all straight-sided figures except ELLIPSE.

Another sort of odd man out question takes this rather different form:

Q83: Spot the odd man out.

TENDER   FLY   OUT   STOOL
ON   RACK   MY   KING   MAID

There seems to be no obvious link between the objects and the grammatical terms which these words stand for. And so you should be looking round for other kinds of link, links that do not rely on the obvious meaning of the words. The inspiration you need here is to realize that all the items on the list can in fact be prefixed by BAR – making BARFLY, BARTENDER, BARSTOOL, and (sneakily) BARON, BARMY, and BARKING for example. The exception is OUT.

ANAGRAMS

An anagram is where the letters of a word are mixed up. Crossword addicts are used to them. But the IQ tester wants to stretch you a bit more than this and, usually, sorting out the anagram is just the first step towards solving the problem. Such as:

Q84: Spot the odd one out.

> HEPES
> OWC
> ROSEH
> INNUPEG

When you unscramble the letters, you find that the words are the names of animals – sheep, cow, horse, and penguin. Penguin is the odd one out on many counts. The others are all domesticated farm animals, all mammals, all grazing animals.

   The fact that you have to unscramble the letters to make up the words is a good indicator that it is the *meaning* you are being tested on, rather than the number of vowels in the word, its general shape or whatever.

RELATIONSHIPS

The _____ is to _____ question is a mainstay of IQ tests. Sometimes you find numbers or figures in the blanks, but usually it is a word of some sort. So what sort of a relationship are you usually being asked to spot if they are words?

Meaning relationships

The most obvious one is some relationship in the meaning of the words in question. For instance:

Q85: Fill in the blank.

> ANEMOMETER is to WIND
> as CHRONOMETER is to ____.

Not too difficult. An anemometer is an instrument for measuring windspeed. A chronometer is something which measures the passing of TIME. It helps if you were raised in Scotland or still have a smattering of your Latin and Greek, but most people should be able to work it out because, even though ANEMOMETER is an unusual word, CHRONOMETER is fairly commonly seen in advertisements for the most expensive (and the cheapest) sort of watches you can buy.

Form of the word

Sometimes the relationship concerns the form of the word, or fitting in the right grammatical version of some basic root. For instance:

Q86: Fill in the missing word.

GLASS	GLAZE	GLAZIER
PAINT	_____	PAINTER

That question is designed to fool you a little bit, because the answer is (again) PAINT. The first word is the material, the second is what you do with it, the third is the professional person who does it.

Such questions occasionally test your vocabulary as well, such as this one does:

Q87: What is the missing word?

SKULL	CRANIAL
THIGH	FEMORAL
EYE	VISUAL
MOUTH	ORAL
EAR	?

The relationship is pretty obvious, but not everyone knows the word AURAL, and quite a few people are likely to confuse it with

ORAL. Remember that next time somebody hands you the telephone upside down.

Disguised letter questions

Be careful though, because these relationships sometimes turn out to be letter questions rather than proper word-meaning questions:

Q88:   Fill in the missing word.

        RATS are to LIVE as EVIL is to ____.

The only answer that makes any sense is that the words make up a palindrome – something that reads the same both forwards and backwards – so that STAR is the solution. Actually this would not in practice be a very good IQ test question because the palindrome it comes from is fairly familiar to people:

        RATS LIVE ON NO EVIL STAR

So we end the word-question section with a warning that some word problems might turn out to be letter problems, just as we ended the letter-question section with the opposite injunction. Small world, isn't it?

WORDS QUIZ

And now it is time to get into practice with another selection of questions.

The answers are on page 160.

Q89: Which is the odd one out?

                NNOODL
                KVAKYREJI
                MORE
                KER NOWY
                OATWAT
                RIDDAM
                SCWOOM

Q90: Which is the odd one out?

   VERY   PET   TON   PING   OX   PORT

Q91: What is the word which finishes the first word outside the brackets and starts the second?

   BORDER(_ _ _ _)AGE

Q92: Who is the odd man out?

   Newton and his Physics
   Mozart and his operas
   Cato and his Epistles
   Schubert and his Unfinished
   Smith and his Economics
   Keats and his Muse
   Dodgson and his Fantasy

Q93: What word means roughly the same as the two given words?

   IRATE |_ _ _ _ _| TRAVERSE

Q94: Complete the sentence:

   SQUARE is to CUBE
   as _____ is to DISK

Q95: Underline the word which means roughly the same as TEMPT.

   allure   intrigue   suggest   cajole   entice

Q96: Spot the odd one out.

   COUNT   BOX
   TRAIN   FLY
   RAIL   FIDDLE
   CITY

Q97: Underline the word which means nearly the opposite of APPROACH.

depart   away   leave   diminish   recede

Q98: What is the word that makes new words with each of the prefixes listed?

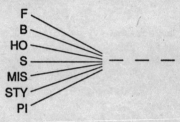

CHAPTER FOURTEEN

FIGURE QUESTIONS

IQ testers like questions that rely on diagrams because they are more 'culture fair' than other types of question. They do not rely so heavily on general knowledge or the sort of literacy and numeracy that you learn – or do not learn – in school. So they crop up to an increasing extent in IQ tests today and some IQ tests use nothing but diagram questions.

This is a slight snag for the IQ booster, because there are many different kinds of diagram question and it is very easy to invent more. Often there are no simple patterns that you can teach yourself to look out for, as you can in numerical series questions.

However, there are a number of general types of diagram question that you do see over and over again and it is certainly worth going through them now.

ODD MAN OUT

Quite often you are presented with a number of diagrams and asked to say which is the odd one out. There are two main possibilities here.

Orientation problems

Take this example of the first group:

Q99: Which is the odd one out?

Often in such questions, the same figure repeats, but is shown in different orientations. Then among these is one figure which is slightly different from all the others, although it may look the same superficially. You have to twist your mind round all the different orientations and work out which is the figure that is slightly different from the repeated figure. In this case, D is the one, because the square and the triangle are the opposite way round in all the others.

Such questions are relatively easy, although some people have difficulty figuring out the different orientations. (Interestingly, men are better than women – which *might* explain all those squabbles over the quality of map-reading that is a feature of Sunday afternoon drives.) More difficult, though, are the questions where you have to find the rule which links different figures.

Finding the rule

In this version of the odd man out question, there is some rule which unites all the figures except one. You have to find which one transgresses the rule. For example:

Q100: Which is the odd one out?

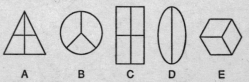

All the figures are divided up; no exception there. They are divided into different numbers of bits, so there is no reason to find any one of them more exceptional than the others on that score. Some have straight edges, some curved. So what can be the rule? Well, on closer inspection you see that each figure, apart from A, is divided into a number of *identical* pieces. None of the four pieces in A is identical to any of the others, so that is the odd one out.

Mixtures

Sometimes a rule question involves a bit of orientational fathoming-out as well:

Q101: Which is the odd one out?

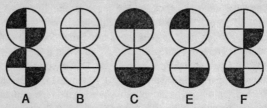

A   B   C   E   F

In this question, the answer seems obvious enough once you have discovered it. All the figures, except one, look the same when you turn them upside-down. F is the exception.

Odd men out

Sometimes you might be asked to identify more than one oddball. Often it is just an orientation job:

Q102: Which are the three odd men out?

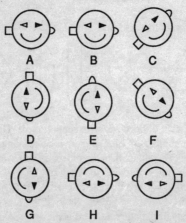

A   B   C

D   E   F

G   H   I

Here the faces are identical, it is just the shape of the ears that changes, so that the odd ones out are D, E, and H. Although these three are similar, they are unlike the other six; and since you were asked to find three oddballs, these must be the ones.

It may not just be orientation, of course. You may have to pick out two or more oddballs from a series of different figures where there is some rule uniting them. However, such contortions could prove rather difficult and you are unlikely to see them in an IQ test. Test-takers are also unnervingly good at working out alternative justifications to pick a completely different set through the application of some quite different rule that the test designer had not thought of.

Not strictly a figure question (or is it?) but this might give the flavour of this kind of task:

Q103: Which are the three odd ones out?

M N O
P Q R
S T U

The answer is M, N, and T. It is nothing to do with the sequence of letters, which is straightforward; so it must be something about the letters themselves. The fact that they are in sanserif type is something of a giveaway too. The only way in which three letters differ from the other six is that M, N, and T comprise entirely straight lines (yes, that old one again), whereas the others contain curves.

FIGURE SERIES

Sometimes you are presented with a number of diagrams and invited to select the figure which would come next.

You don't have to be an artist to figure out this sort of test question: usually, the answer involves picking out one from a set of alternatives that are already drawn for you.

Sequence questions

Questions like this are almost always sequence questions, as in the following case:

Q104: Which of the five figures listed below fits into the blank space?

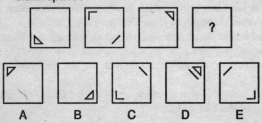

This example from Thierry Carabin looks hard to fathom until you start imagining it as a regular progression, like a series question. Then you see that the inner line of the triangle breaks off and revolves anti-clockwise from one frame to the next; while the outer lines revolve clockwise. If this pattern is followed, E would be the next in the series.

What makes this particular question so hard is that we tend to see figures as whole figures rather than as a number of component parts. We assume the components must be something else completely, so we miss the link between one frame and the next. It is a point to look out for in diagram questions.

Pattern prediction

In other cases, again, there is some rule or pattern which all the given diagrams follow, and only one of the potential answers fits the blank. This question illustrates the sort of thing:

Q105: Which of the five figures comes next?

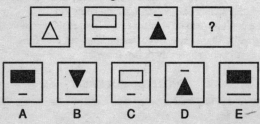

This problem, again from Thierry Carabin, relies more on building up a pattern than on a series. A shaded figure means a shorter line; the same figure takes the same position above or below the line; there is one blank and one shaded figure of each sort. A, the figure with the shaded figure oblong above a short line, is the obvious one to be next in the pattern.

PROGRESSIVE MATRICES

Very popular in IQ tests today are what are called progressive matrices. Try this one:

Q106: Pick out the figure which completes the given pattern.

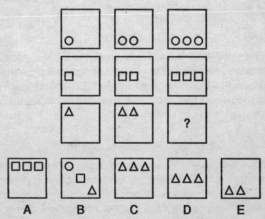

A   B   C   D   E

Usually, these progressive matrices are figure questions where nine figures are set out in three rows of three, with the last blank. Your task is to pick the one which fits from (usually five) given possibilities.

The rule in the question above is that the type of figure inside the box – circle, square, and triangle – changes as you move down from the top row to the bottom. So does the position of the figures with respect to the frame. As you move left to right, the number of the figures increases from one to three. Thus we need an answer with the following conditions: triangles, three in number, top of the box, giving C as the only answer.

Although very simple, this is typical of how this sort of problem, called a progressive matrix, works. There are regular progressions of some sort in evidence as you work from left to right and from top to bottom. Work out all the progressions and you can spot the right answer from the alternatives.

The 'culture fair' aspects of this type of question make it a staple of modern IQ tests. Designing questions to fit it has become something of an art form, so there are many different varieties. It is hard, therefore, to prepare yourself for all eventualities.

However, there are a number of quite common forms of progressive matrix questions and the trick is to spot which sort you are dealing with. So let's look at a selection.

Orientation

Sometimes, the progression might simply involve a systematic change in the orientation of some figure or figures – say, a triangle turning steadily clockwise from left to right and anticlockwise from top to bottom (yes, it *is* possible, and in fact it is quite common, so give it a try).

Number in a row or column

On other occasions, there is a pattern to detect. Very common is the pattern where each item in the grid contains a different number of features, but those numbers are repeated in each row or each column (or in rows *and* columns). The question above showing one, then two, then three circles or squares or triangles gives you an idea of this sort of thing.

On similar lines but perhaps a shade more difficult, is where each row and each column contains the same total number of some feature, though the particular number that some individual item possesses does not necessarily follow a 1-2-3-style pattern. For example:

Q107: Which of the labelled figures will complete the pattern?

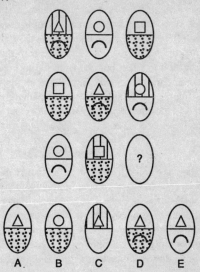

The items in this matrix look a bit like faces and that is not uncommon – dressing up the questions to look interesting is a way in which test psychologists amuse themselves during the coffee break. In this case, the first two rows and first two columns each contain a triangle, a circle and a square in the top of the figure, so we should expect the row and column containing the missing figure to do the same. But that only narrows the possible answers down to four possibilities – A, C, D, and E.

Looking further, we see that only one figure in those same rows and columns features vertical shading, so we would expect this to be repeated in the third row and the third column. Both of those have the shading already, so it can't be C. Another possibility bites the dust.

Then we see that in each of the first two rows and two columns there are *two* drooping mouths. Only an answer with a drooping mouth would complete this pattern for the third row and the third column, so now we are down to D and E. Soldier on.

Lastly we note that the first two rows and columns also have two speckled areas. Figure D is the only one of our remaining alternatives which fits this pattern, so that must be the right answer.

Notice that the matrix gives you a lot of clues – there is not only a pattern from left to right, but one from top to bottom. You can pretty well count on this being so in virtually all matrix questions. Unlike this figure, it may not be the *same* pattern, so be careful. But at least you have a couple of shots to work out the right progression and the right answer.

Rotations

Instead of the trick being to find some particular number of elements on each row and each column, it may be that you are faced with some sort of sequence rule – a line getting longer as you move rightward, thicker as you move down and that sort of thing.

A favourite sequence concept is where some feature of each item in the pattern rotates according to some regular rule. And common among these rotational questions is the clock:

Q108: Which clock comes next in the series?

This is a fairly straightforward clock question. The hour hand moves forward two hours as you move from left to right, and it moves forward one hour as you travel from top to bottom. The minute hand goes forward by forty-five minutes (or, if you like, *backwards* by fifteen minutes) as you go from left to right, and forward by fifteen minutes (or . . . well, you know) as you travel from top to bottom. So the correct clock to complete the pattern is the one set at three o'clock.

Trickier versions: These questions can be much trickier, however. Sometimes there is an hour hand moving at quite another speed entirely which means you have to do yet another calculation. Sometimes the hands do not move in regular intervals but in increasing or decreasing ones: usually (because you have only three figures in a row or column to establish the pattern) the interval is straightforward – say, one hour, then two. In really sneaky versions the hour hand will move to where the minute hand was before. In amazingly sneaky questions, the two hands are the same length and you have to work out which is which. And if the design is done in a square box instead of a circle, you might not even recognize it as a clock question at all.

Obscuring rotations

If you can imagine a clock question where the hour hand *obscures* a minute hand of equal length, you will see that such a question could be quite hard to work out.

Questions where one feature of each item – a clock hand or a coloured panel – rotates and sometimes obscures what must be underneath it are quite widely used, however. Of course, they *are* reckoned to be hard and so tend to appear only in the more difficult tests, or as questions to sort out the high-fliers in more general tests. But at least if you know what to look for, you might be better able to do them or avoid them!

An example of this complex form of rotational question might be this one:

Q109: Which figure completes the pattern?

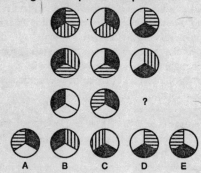

This one is pretty sneaky, because the black panel moves round, but in doing so it obscures the ones underneath it. The white and the horizontally and vertically striped segments stay where they are. It's made harder by the fact that in the last row there are two white segments. So when the black bit moves round again, another white is exposed, giving E as the right answer.

Additions and subtractions

Sometimes you find that features in the first two items add or subtract to give you the last figure in the row or column. Such as:

Q110: Which figure comes next?

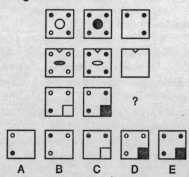

The simple rule here is that features of the same colour reinforce, while features of different colours drop out. So on the last row, the corner box drops out, as does the spot at the top right-hand corner, giving figure A as the correct answer.

Now if you can imagine that sort of thing going on while some of the features are rotating at the same time, you really do have the sort of perverse mind it takes to set puzzle questions. You might occasionally find something of that difficulty in an IQ test, but luckily they are very rare!

OTHER QUESTIONS

The other sorts of questions might as well be lumped together.

Dominoes

Dominoes, shapes with upper and lower boxes, can appear in progressive matrices, but usually they are sequence-type questions. And usually, the point is that there are different rules afoot in each half:

Q111: What domino comes next?

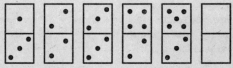

Don't look too hard for the rule in this example, or you will probably come up with another answer! But the obvious one is that the numbers on the top deck of the dominoes increase by one each time, while the bottom ones alternate from three to two and back again. So the last domino must have six dots in the top deck and two in the bottom.

Analogies

We have seen in another context the sort of question that is phrased as 'A is to B as C is to ?' and you can do the same with figures. To take a simple example:

Q112: Identify the figure which completes the relationship.

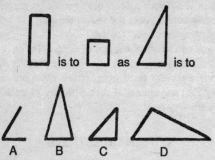

The second one of each pair is just a shortened version of the first – no figure fits except C in this case.

There can be several such relationships. Quite common are those where, to get the second figure in each pair, the first is:

●   rotated or inverted
●   elongated in some direction
●   placed next to its mirror image
●   partially rotated or reversed.

You name it, you can have it.

Of course, you can be even more crafty with these figure relationships and it doesn't always pay to be thinking only in two dimensions. Take this one:

Q113: Which figure completes the relation?

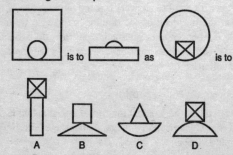

Phew! That one appeared in *Test Your IQ* (Pan Books, 1983) and it is very nasty. The answer is that the first of each pair is two shapes seen from the top, while the second of the pair is the same shapes seen from end on. Only C, a pyramid sitting on the edge of a lens, would give you the right view from the top and the side. But don't expect three-dimensional questions like that in the average IQ test!

Which shapes fit?

Sometimes the question is just a sort of jigsaw puzzle that you have to fit together, such as this one:

Q114: Which four pieces can be put together to form a square?

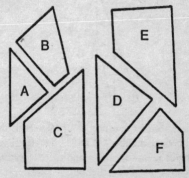

The answer is pieces C, D, E, and F. This is one of those questions you have to work out for yourself. If you have bought this book, feel free to cut the bits out and try it, but those who have borrowed it had better resort to photocopying!

You will find simple versions of this sort of thing in IQ tests from time to time, but generally speaking the more intricate varieties are reserved for puzzle magazines and books.

How many shapes?

Most people know from their comic-book days the annoying sort of question where you are asked to say how many squares or triangles are in a particular pattern, and they do appear in IQ tests from time to time.

Nevertheless, these questions again fall more generally within the jurisdiction of puzzle books and magazines than IQ tests, partly because it is so easy to make a mistake and overlook part of the answer, however intelligent you might be.

The trick with these questions, of course, is to know that, as well as the obvious squares or triangles, the smaller ones fit together to produce bigger ones which must also be counted. Take this one from Philip Carter and Ken Russell:

Q115: How many triangles are there in the following figure?

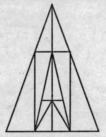

The authors classify this question as of 'standard' difficulty. But did you get the right number? It is 23 triangles. Remember that there are triangles within triangles and some very nasty triangles made up from three or four smaller ones.

So you see, these questions can quite easily end up with you having to spot dozens of triangles, or squares, or whatever it might be, and missing just one means you have got the question wrong, which is why they are really on the boundary between IQ questions and puzzles.

Dice

Dice questions can be a real brain-teaser. You are given a glimpse of three or four sides of a die, and asked to identify what is on the other face. The faces can be dots or figures.

If they are dots, the question will often tell you that the dots on opposite faces of a die always add up to seven (if your grandmother always beats you at backgammon, it's worth checking hers out – there are some very crooked grandmothers around these days).

Usually though, it is a pattern which is involved. This is a typical dice question:

Q116: Here are four different views of the same cube. What design is missing from the blank face?

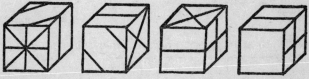

Well, it's the Union Jack design once again, the same design that was facing you in the first picture.

Once again, such questions do occur in tests from time to time but belong more to the category of puzzle problems.

So let's move on to the puzzles in the next chapter. But first, you might like to sharpen your wits on some of the following figure problems.

VISUAL QUIZ

Q117: Here are four drawings of the same toy alphabet cube. Draw what should appear on the face that is left blank.

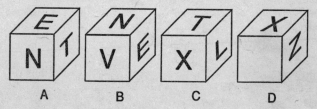

A   B   C   D

Q118: Which figure completes the analogy?

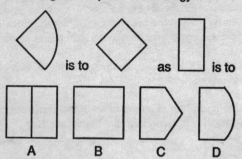

Q119: Draw the domino which completes the series.

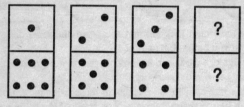

Q120: Which of the labelled figures completes the pattern?

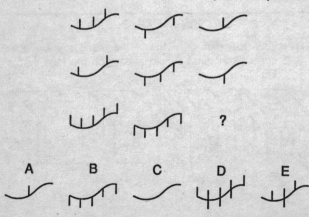

Q121: Which fish completes the pattern?

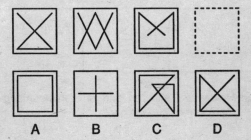

Q122: Which figure completes the series?

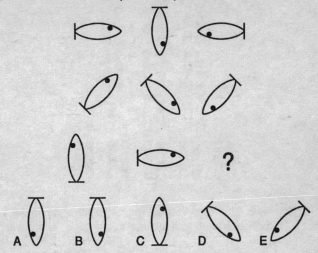

Q123: Which figure is the odd one out?

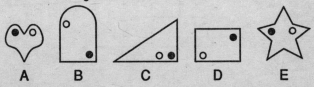

Q124: Which pair of footballers completes the pattern?

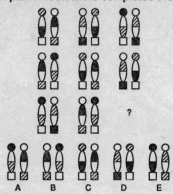

Q125: Two of these shapes will fit together to make a perfect square without leaving any gaps. Which two?

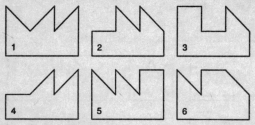

Q126: How many squares and how many triangles are there in the figure below?

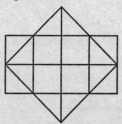

CHAPTER FIFTEEN

LOGIC PUZZLES

Logic puzzles come in all shapes and sizes. Usually they are not suitable for IQ tests precisely because they require quite a bit of working out and it is too easy to make mistakes.

It is impossible to go through the full range of logic puzzles that exist today and indeed, professional puzzlers are inventing new ones every day. A few of the most common are rewarding to look at, however.

OVERLAPPING SETS

The first group features questions where some population is divided into different segments, perhaps overlapping, and where you have to chart the consequences. Consider this one:

Q127: All tyres are rubber. All rubber is flexible. Some rubber is black. So which two of the following five statements are necessarily true?

    (a)   All tyres are flexible and black.
    (b)   All tyres are black.
    (c)   Only some tyres are rubber.
    (d)   All tyres are flexible.
    (e)   All tyres are flexible and rubber.

The answer is that (d) and (e) are necessarily true. Of course, it might well be that in practice all tyres happen to be black, but you cannot reason that out for sure from the statements you were given at the beginning.

One way to work out the answers to questions of this sort is to draw the various groupings as overlapping circles. Then, by seeing which circles might or must overlap, you can see how many people must fall into each different category. In this case, your chart might look like this:

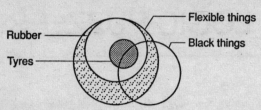

Thus, all the tyres are on the area of rubber things, the rubber things are all on the area occupied by flexible things. Some of the rubber area is on the black area, but we don't know exactly how much. And we leave open the possibility that some black things are not flexible, as we must do when the question does not tell us anything about it.

These overlapping circles, or sets, provide a good technique to help you with jumbled syllogisms (as logicians call them) such as 'some sheep are white; some men are white; therefore some men are sheep.' It may be true metaphorically, but resorting to the technique shows that it does not have to be correct in point of fact. The populations of 'sheep' and 'men' do not have to overlap.

JUMBLED SENTENCE STRINGS

Another common puzzle is where there is a sentence strung out through a matrix of letters. This is an example:

Q128: This grid contains a short sentence which can be read by finding the starting letter and moving one space at a time horizontally or vertically (but not diagonally). No letter is used more than once. What is the sentence?

H	A	E	A	H	O
O	R	S	E	S	R
E	A	R	M	I	N
S	H	O	Y	K	G
R	O	F	M	O	D

It is often a shrewd move to start with the unusual letters in questions of this kind – letters such as Y and K for example. In this case, the familiar sentence comes from Shakespeare's *Richard III* – 'A horse, a horse, my kingdom for a horse.'

MAZES

Usually a maze is straightforward enough. You have to get from A to B, and only one route will do it. Occasionally you get an odd version, however, for example:

Q129: In the maze shown below, what is the least number of lines which must be crossed in getting from A to B?

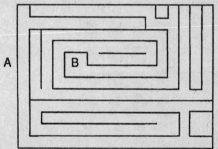

Sneaky, huh? The answer is a humble *one*, and with that information you can work out the exact route yourself!

ARITHMETICAL COMPUTATIONS

Usually involving money or ages, arithmetic puzzles are a staple of every comic. A typical example would be:

Q130: Mary and Jane went shopping together for sweets with 66p between them. Mary started out with 6p more than Jane, but spent twice as much as Jane. Mary finished up with two-thirds as much money as Jane. How much did Jane spend?

The answer is 12p. It helps to know a little algebra – which is no more than putting 'x' or 'y' in the place of the unknown quantities so that you can work out the sums and fill them in at the end.

APPLES AND BANANAS

Grids of different objects – geometrical shapes or fruit, for example – whose rows and columns add up to numerical scores, are a well-known puzzle. Often, they appear in magazines and newspapers supplied by the high-IQ society MENSA. This one is typical:

Q131: Each of the five fruits in this grid has a different value. The numbers shown represent the totals for the various rows and columns. What is the missing number?

Often, as in this case, you do not really have to resort to complicated simultaneous equations involving five unknowns to get the answer. Whatever the value of each fruit, the total of all the fruit in the grid must be the same whether you add it up lengthways or sideways. So add up all the numbers at the bottom, to get the total value of the fruit in the grid. Then add up all the numbers on the right – which gives you the total for three out of the four rows. So the difference – 67 – must be the total of the remaining row.

OTHER VARIETIES

There are plenty of other varieties of puzzle question, too many to list. But most of them you won't find in an IQ test. So relax, and have a go at the following questions just for practice.

LOGIC QUIZ

Q132: Of the pupils in the class:

— 50% have black hair;
— 25% have blond hair;
— 33% are girls; and
— 67% are boys.

Which of the following statements are definitely true?

(a) The blond-haired pupils are all boys.
(b) Some boys have black hair.
(c) Some blond-haired pupils are girls.
(d) Both girls and boys have black hair.
(e) Some girls have blond hair, some black.

Q133: Among these letters there is a coiled sentence. However, three of the letters are not used. What is the hidden sentence?

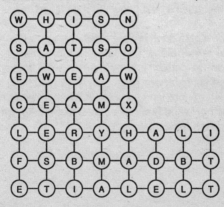

Q134: I bought some plates at a jumble sale. When I got them home, I found that two-thirds were chipped, half were cracked, and a quarter were both chipped and cracked. Only two had no chips or cracks at all. How many plates did I buy altogether?

Q135: A wall is to be covered with 36 tiles arranged as shown. Only black and white tiles are available, and there must be no straight rows (horizontal, vertical, or diagonal) of three adjacent white tiles. Subject to this rule, what is the smallest number of black tiles required?

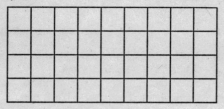

Q136: I tried to repair my clock. Now the hour hand works perfectly, but the minute hand runs anticlockwise at constant speed, crossing the hour hand every 80 minutes. If my clock shows the correct time at 6.30, when does it next show the right time?

Q137: The sights on my rifle are out of alignment, and it hits the target below and to the left of where I aim. If I want to correct this by adjusting the foresight (the one at the far end of the barrel) would I have to move it left or right, and up or down? And if I were to adjust the backsight (the one nearest to my eye), which way would it have to move?

CHAPTER SIXTEEN

LESSONS IN TEST TECHNIQUE

There are some tips that will help you in every test, not just in IQ tests. Really they should be taught in school because knowing them can give students a big boost in confidence and perhaps even a modest boost on their examination score.

RULE ONE

The first rule is to read the question and know what you are being asked to do. Many students spend a quarter of their allotted time in examinations trying to answer a question that they have completely misinterpreted. A brilliant answer to the wrong question still earns you no marks.

In written examinations, remember that the question is there only to reveal the breadth and depth of your knowledge and understanding. So don't go on and on about only one part of the subject: work out the range of relevant topics that the examiner might be interested in, and say less about more of them.

In IQ tests you do not have that problem because the answers are usually designed to be written quickly and are normally just a single word, letter, or number. But if you are aware of what sort of relationships the question is testing, you will arrive at the answer much more quickly.

RULE TWO

Always put down something, especially in tests using multiple-choice questions. It is very rare indeed that marks are knocked off for wrong answers in examinations and in IQ testing it probably never happens. One thing is certain: a blank space does not earn you any marks at all.

So if you have a reasonable idea of what the answer might be, write it down. You can always put some sort of identifying mark after your answer so that you can return to the problem should you have time at the end.

Otherwise, it is worth writing in guesswork answers as you go through the test because you might not have time to go back to the question and work it out properly. But if you have a last few seconds spare at the end or, when you have done all the questions you think you can do, a few random guesswork answers will not do any harm.

This is especially true on questions where there are only a few possible answers. In matrix questions where you cannot expect people to draw a complicated diagram, for example, the answer must be chosen from (say) six numbered figures. On a test of thirty questions, then, chance alone would give you a score of five. Not much, but better than leaving it blank.

Technically, psychologists regard this as cheating and in the test instructions they may even tell you not to guess randomly. But generally there is no penalty for doing it and, in any case, would they know?

RULE THREE

The next rule is not to spend too long on any one question. In written school examinations, there might be a hundred marks to be scored on four questions. Usually that means that twenty-five is the maximum you can score on any one. A perfect answer on that question and nothing at all on the others will still get you only twenty-five marks. And usually, the time you spend getting the couple of extra marks on your best question could be much better used showing that you know *something*, at least, about the others. So it is best to divide your time equally between the questions.

IQ tests have a rather different construction, but much the same rule holds. The questions on IQ tests have to be quick to do because the test attempts to summarize your ability on many different subjects at various levels of difficulty. Some are harder, some easier, but it is a very unusual IQ question which takes a long time to solve. A bit of persistence may be rewarded but generally you will find that you are approaching the question wrongly if it takes too long. You might be better to look for another approach or to move on to others that will boost your score more quickly.

Pace yourself throughout the test, so that with luck you will be on the last question as the final seconds tick away.

RULE FOUR

If you have time at the end, check your solutions. IQ test questions are designed to have only one correct answer – though sometimes the tester overlooks a few odd alternatives. If you were unhappy about an answer on the first try, have another look at it when you reach the end.

If by any chance you do see two solutions to the same question, and you are pretty sure that both are correct, write them both down. If you think both are correct but one is better, write that one down first and put the second as an alternative in brackets afterwards.

You won't be able to hedge your bets this way (don't try giving the answer to a matrix question as '1 or 2 or 3 or 4 or 5 or 6'). Generally, IQ test questions are designed to have only one correct answer, but even experienced testers can make mistakes, and candidates quite often come up with perfectly reasonable alternatives.

So it is worth putting down an alternative if you are sure it is just as good. The one you put down as an alternative could well be the answer which the test designer has put down on the score sheet. Examiners are usually a pretty reasonable bunch and they like to check the construction of the test on live subjects, so if the examiner agrees that your first choice is also defensible, you should get the mark (and maybe earn some unacknowledged gratitude).

RULE FIVE

Be refreshed. This is even more true on tests of mental ability than it is on written examinations. If you're suffering a headache from overdoing it the night before, you simply will not be able to think IQ problems out efficiently.

And it is also best not to do more than one IQ test per day. You need time for your thoughts about one set of problems to settle down before you attack another set, so get a good night's sleep between. Too recent a memory of one group of IQ questions can actually interfere with your ability to do another set that may demand a slightly different approach.

So if you have just worked through some of the exercises in this book, put it away and do not attempt the next test until tomorrow. You will probably do much better as a result.

RULE SIX

Practice. In school examinations, there is nothing better than trying yourself out on a bunch of past papers before you sit the big one. If nothing else, it helps you understand a little of how the examiners think.

In IQ tests too, you quickly improve by doing a few tests. Fortunately, today there are a fair number of IQ test collections available on sale to the general public. And there are plenty of other books containing logic puzzles and reasoning questions that are not sorted into tests but are just meant for fun and practice.

Why not try a few of them before you go on?

Strongly recommended are H. J. Eysenck's Pelican classics, containing standardized tests of different kinds, *Know Your Own IQ* (Penguin Books, 1962) and *Check Your Own IQ* (Penguin Books, 1966).

Then there is Glenn Wilson's entertaining Futura book, *Improve Your IQ* (Macdonald Futura, 1974), containing roughly 130 typical IQ questions, good for coaching. For those with a smattering of French, Thierry Carabin's *Testez Votre Logique* (Orthez, 1988) is good. More to the puzzle end of the spectrum, Philip Carter and Ken Russell have collaborated on two Javelin books *Take the IQ Challenge* (Javelin, 1987), which use a star system to divide the questions between 'standard' (*) and 'appallingly difficult' (****).

And you should not be surprised to find recommended here *Test Your IQ* by Eamonn Butler and Madsen Pirie, published by Pan Books, 1983.

As a final measure, look over the sixty items in the first test you did earlier, and check how the answers are derived. Learning from your mistakes is one of the best ways of acquiring any new skill!

PART FOUR

RE-TEST
YOUR IQ

CHAPTER SEVENTEEN

GETTING THE MEASURE OF YOUR IQ BOOST

Now it is time to run through another set of IQ questions to see whether the coaching you went through in the earlier chapters really boosted your IQ. We will check this using another IQ test, very similar to the first one which you took at the outset.

BE PREPARED

First, don't do the test if you have just finished going through the coaching exercises – particularly if it is late at night by now. Give yourself a good night's sleep and do it tomorrow. And even then, wait until you are feeling awake and alert before you start the test.

Second, do look through the answers to the first test once again – not just to see where you went wrong, but to help you understand the mind of the test compiler.

BEGINNING THE TEST

As before, you need a good clock or watch because you have to time yourself precisely.

If you can find somebody to time you, well and good; but don't let them look over your shoulder or put you off.

Like the first test, and most IQ tests, the answer to each question is a simple number, word, or letter.

Again, there are no sneaky or misleading questions. They are all straightforward reasoning tasks, though of course some are more difficult than others.

You can write your answers down in the book, or on a separate piece of paper. If you are using a piece of paper, you might like to put the question numbers 1–60 down the left-hand side, so that you can put your answers next to them.

There are sixty questions and you have forty-five minutes to do them.

Do all the questions before turning to the answers at the back of the book. The answers can be found on page 163.

When you are comfortable and prepared, check your starting time and begin.

You have 45 minutes to complete this test

1   Which of the six given figures completes the pattern?

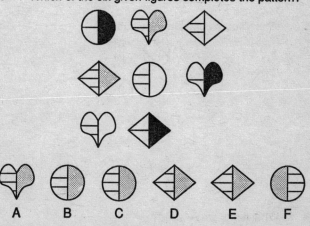

A   B   C   D   E   F

2   What is the missing word?

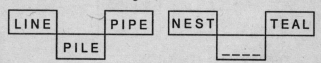

| LINE | | PIPE | | NEST | | TEAL |
| PILE | | | | | ____ | |

3   What number comes next?

1   12   3   11   5   10   7

4   What three-letter word can be prefixed by any of the letters on the left to make new words?

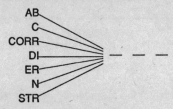

AB
C
CORR
DI
ER
N
STR

– – –

5   Which figure completes the pattern?

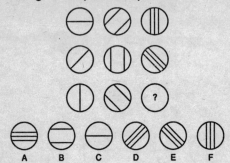

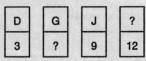

A   B   C   D   E   F

6   What items are missing?

D	G	J	?
3	?	9	12

7   What are the missing numbers?

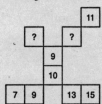

8 Which numbers come next in the series?

| 2 | 5 | | 3 | 4 | | 4 | 3 | | ? | ? |

9 What is the missing letter?

10 What number is missing?

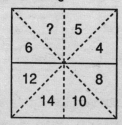

11 What letters complete the square?

```
T  O  P
O  D  ?
?  E  A
```

12 What word means nearly the same as the two given words?

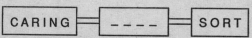

CARING — _ _ _ _ — SORT

13   Which figure comes next?

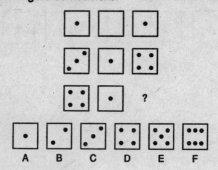

14   How far is BERLIN?

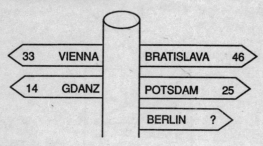

15   Which are the odd two out?

WEIGH	PEAL	RAYS	WAY	PAIN	PANE
RAISE	RUFF	ROUGH	PEEL	BAWL	PRIZE
BALL	BOW	PRISE	BOUGH	WALL	WOW

16   Identify the missing number.

2	6	9
5	19	25
1	4	?

17 What is the missing word?

R		D	
S	T	E	W
	U		X

V		M	
_	_	_	_
	J		F

18 What should go in the blank space?

19 What three-letter word completes the first word and starts the second?

S H _ _ _ T H

20 Which figure fits the series?

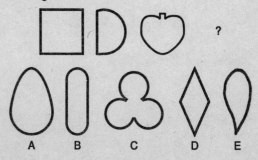

A   B   C   D   E

21   Which is the odd one out?

      RAT   FOX   DOG   CAT   OWL   COW

22   Which of the four given figures completes the pattern?

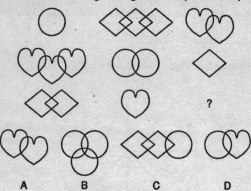

A   B   C   D

23   Which letter completes the series?

      A   D   H   M   S   ?

24   Which is the odd man out?

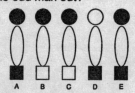

25   What word fits in the space?

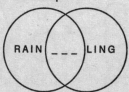

26 Which letter comes next?

C H L O Q ?

27 What is the missing number?

8   5   11
6   17   1
10   2   ?

28 What is the missing word that completes the pattern?

LAMB <BLED> DOLE
ARAB <____> EARL

29 Which of the six given figures completes the pattern?

A   B   C   D   E   F

30   What is the missing number?

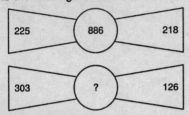

31   Insert the number that completes the relationship.

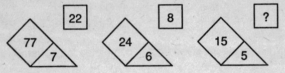

32   Which word means nearly the same as the words outside the circle?

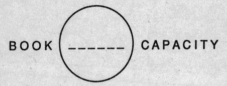

BOOK   CAPACITY

33   Which figure completes the pattern?

34 Which is the odd one out?

LALH
NETCHIK
BROODEM
KARP
CITTA

35 What is the missing word?

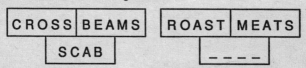

CROSS BEAMS   ROAST MEATS
SCAB   _ _ _ _

36 Here are two sides of the same die. The number of dots on opposite sides of a die add up to seven. How many dots belong on the black face of this one?

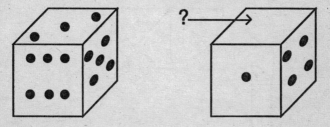

37 What is the missing number?

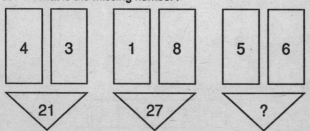

38   What is the missing letter?

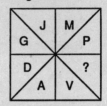

39   Which letter comes next?

A E J P _

40   What are the missing letters?

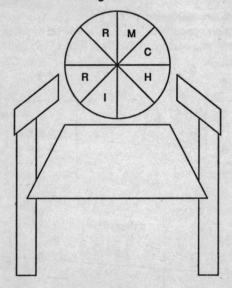

41   What is the missing letter?

| Y | ? | I | D | A |

42   Which figure completes the pattern?

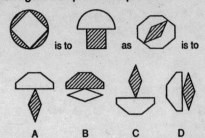

43   Which is the odd one out?

HONEST   MEAN   SLY   ASLEEP   VIRTUOUS

44   What is the missing number?

1	0.5
2	4.0
3	13.5
4	?
5	62.5

45   Which figure completes the pattern?

46   Identify the missing numbers.

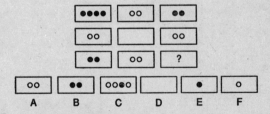

47   Which is the odd one out?

    WERBODAR
    PUMMS
    RAICH
    BELAT

48   Which letter comes next?

    O T T F F S S E N T E ?

49   Identify the missing number.

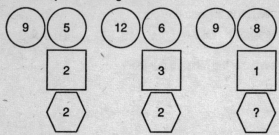

50   Which figure completes the pattern?

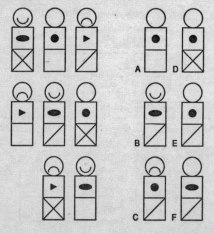

51   Identify the missing number.

20	10	4	16
35	17.5	?	28

52   Which of the given words fits in the box?

AUNT	SON	UNCLE	PAL	COUSIN
A	B	C	D	E

53   Which of the given figures completes the pattern?

54   What is the missing number?

1045	17	1123

917	?	203

55   Which of the given figures completes the pattern?

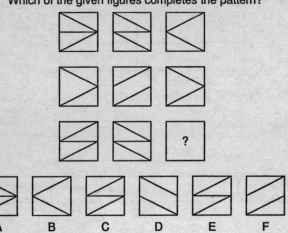

56   Identify the odd one out.

CABLED
ODE
AGHAST
CHIME
ANON
TOPIARY
ASTERISK
ATTUNED

57   What is the missing word?

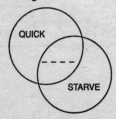

58 Identify the missing number.

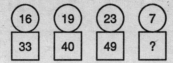

59 Find the missing letters.

60 Which word is most nearly the opposite of HURT?

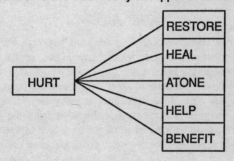

CHAPTER NINETEEN

BOOSTED YOUR IQ?

Can you see any improvement in your performance between the two tests?

If you can, give yourself a pat on the back for having boosted your IQ. Technically speaking you cannot really tell very much from a person's IQ score between one test and another, but why not take the credit anyway? It's good for your morale and that might help you to do even better in your next test.

Of course, this book has not really made you a brainier or a better person but perhaps now you are closer to fulfilling your genuine potential on IQ tests. With a bit more practice on a few more tests you might see your score edging up even more.

DON'T WORRY

Is your score actually worse? Hopefully not, but don't worry. That often happens and it does not mean that you have become dimmer as a result of all this hard work.

Psychologists hesitate to mention it, but there is quite a bit of vagueness about IQ scores. Your score on any one can easily vary seven points one way or the other from the average you clock up on a string of tests. So on a bad day you could well be fourteen or fifteen points down on your best performance.

Remember too that as well as being imprecise, the IQ figure is only a statistic, a summary number. It tries to lump together some measure of your ability on several different kinds of question, requiring different skills of reasoning and memory and of varying degrees of difficulty. It may be that the particular mix of questions just wasn't one which you are good at.

NO IMPROVEMENT?

Did you end up with pretty much the same score as when you began?

The obvious question to ask here is are you a habitual puzzler who has seen it all before? If so, you probably have very little to learn and it is doubtful whether you can boost your IQ any further.

People do get better as they take more IQ tests or with a bit of coaching. But it only takes about three to five goes at IQ tests before you become about as good as you are likely to get. You might even get your IQ score up ten or fifteen points with practice. But do more than a few tests and your improvement tails off quickly. Eventually you don't improve further at all – or if you do, it is by such a small amount that no IQ test could hope to measure it. You have reached what the psychologists call 'saturation'.

That is why professional IQ testers often give people several 'dummy' tests first before the crucial ones.

It is also worth mentioning here that an IQ test of sixty items is reckoned to be quite a long one. Some questions in the test are inevitably going to be rather similar to others, giving you an opportunity for practice even within the test itself. When you have found an effective approach to one question, you can apply the same technique more quickly when faced with a roughly similar one. Having benefited already from this practice effect within Test One, you may not improve much further as you take Test Two.

THE REAL TEST

Hopefully, though, you should have shown at least some improvement as you have learnt more about IQ tests and practised on them with this book. The important thing is not what IQ score you achieve – because you should always take such figures with a pinch of salt – but *whether* it improved.

And the real test is not even this, but whether you felt more prepared and confident during the second test than you did in the first. With that understanding and confidence, you are likely to do better in future IQ tests than you could without it.

Why not try to get your confidence up even further? All IQ tests are different and will give different results but you will have fun doing them now that you know a little about what to expect. And at least the process will get you firmly into the swing of doing reasoning questions.

PART FIVE

ANSWERS

CHAPTER TWENTY

ANSWERS
TO TEST ONE

When checking your answers to this test, you might find that you have come up with an alternative answer and explanation that seems just as good as the ones given. You may count these as correct provided that your reasoning could not lead to any other solution being correct, and is not unnecessarily convoluted as seen against a straightforward explanation.

When you have checked your answers, add up the number of correct solutions you obtained. You can translate your score into a rough estimate of your IQ using the chart on page 168.

1: FIRE.
2: D. Figures with straight edges are shaded on the left; figures with curved edges are shaded on the right.
3: ATE.
4: 5. Add the second and third numbers, then subtract one, to get the number in the first column.
5: BE. Making ADOBE and BETRAY.
6: C. Each row and each column possesses one figure with square, triangular, or round ears; a smile, frown, or straight expression; and one, two or three stripes on each half of the bow tie.
7: 5. Divide the number in the top left-hand box by the number in the bottom, and halve the result.
8: HEAD. Making BRIDGEHEAD and HEADLAMPS.
9: B. There are one, two, or three circles, diamonds, and triangles in each row and each column.
10: CLOUD. All the others go with COAT.
11: LAST. Take the fifth letter of the first word, the third and fifth of the second word, and the third of the first to form the letters in the missing word.

12: T. The letters of each pair are the same distance from the beginning and the end of the alphabet. Thus G is the same distance from A as T is from Z.

13: D. Each row and column has black, white, and grey areas in each half of the domino; so we need one with the missing elements of grey on the top and black underneath.

14: FURLONG and RATE. The others join to make new words or word pairs: INCH-TAPE, FOOTSTEP, YARD-ARM, CHAINMAIL, MILESTONE, and LEAGUE TABLE.

15: 2. The rows and columns each sum to 32.

16: READS. The word is formed by taking the fourth, third, and first letters of the second word and the fifth and second letters of the first word.

17: A. In each row and column, the spot goes round clockwise, while the triangle spins anticlockwise.

18: 72436. In the code, each letter is represented by a number. The numbers corresponding to the letters T,R,I,P, and E are 7,2,4,3, and 6 respectively.

19: 219. Halve the difference between the numbers in the circles to get the missing number.

20: K. There is an interval of three letters, backwards through the alphabet, on each domino.

21: 6. Add the lower numbers and divide by three.

22: LYSET, an anagram of STYLE. The others are all grammatical items: WORD, PARAGRAPH, SENTENCE, and CLAUSE.

23: A and A. The letters on the screen spell out DATABANK clockwise.

24: Y. In the alphabetical series, the interval between the letters decreases by one each time.

25: PEWS. Letters above the missing ones are one further on in the alphabet, letters below are one behind in the alphabet.

26: 126. Take the cubes of the five numbers at the top, and add one to each.

27: TAILS. Making COCKTAILS and TAILSPIN.

28: C. The frame reverses; the spot changes colour and moves position; the square remains in the same position and of the same colour.

29: SPOKE.

30: G and P. The top series goes backwards through the alphabet in steps of one letter; the bottom series goes backwards in steps of two.

31: D. Dots on top count +1, dots underneath count –1, and rows and columns sum. Thus 2 – 3 = –1, or 1 – 2 = –1.

32: The intervals in the top row increase by one each time, starting at 5; the intervals in the bottom row decrease by one each time, starting at 7.

33: B. Circles count positive, triangles negative; the rows and columns sum. Zero is the only answer.

34: 2. Add the figures in triangles and divide the result into the figure in the circle to reach the figure in the square.

35: SUPPLE. Not AGILE as is often supposed.

36: 24. The numbers in the bottom half of the square are a quarter of those in the corresponding top segments.

37: OFF. Each segment is opposed by its opposite; black-white, sun-moon, no-yes, and on-off.

38: SNOSOKS, an anagram for KNOSSOS, the ancient Cretan city. All the others are modern European countries: AUSTRIA, DENMARK and GERMANY.

39: 39. Treble the top number and subtract 8, 9, 10, and 11.

40: D, standing for DECEMBER. The given letters represent the initial letters of the months in the year.

41: 2. The bottom numbers are twice the top row, minus 1,2,3, and 4.

42: 3. Each box has A, B, or C in the first segment, D, E, or F in the second,, and G,H, or I in the third, with no repeats in any row or column.

43: 18. Add the digits in the outside boxes to get the number in the centre box.

44: B. Similar quarters sum to white in each row and column; dissimilar quarters sum to black.

45: METES. The words in each domino sound like a new word when taken together: SUCCEED and SWEETMEATS.

46: H. With this letter, all the words can now be formed into the pairs BOOKWORM, ARCHBISHOP, PATHWAY, SUIT-CASE, and NUTCRACKER.

47:

7
7

The top deck is a series going up in steps of two; the bottom deck is a series diminishing by one each time.

48: PORT.

49: R and L. The letters spell PARASOL when read clockwise.

50: LOWER. All the others begin with consecutive letters of the alphabet: AB, EF, GH, NO, and TU.

51: 49 and 44. The numbers move down by one between each column, reading from left to right, and up by three between each row, reading from top to bottom.

52: D. The shapes change from left to right, and the shading moves round regularly.

53:

2
B

The top deck increases by four each time, the bottom contains the corresponding letter at that place in the alphabet.

54: CONCUR.

55: B. There are two alternating series. In one, starting with K, each letter is two further on in the alphabet than the preceding one; in the other, starting with H, the letters are two further back each time.

56: 6. There are two alternating series, each diminishing by one each time.

57: B. Ducks A and E are identical, as are C and D. B is not like any other figure.

58: DRAG. Take the fourth and third letters of the right-hand word and the second and first letters of the one on the left in order to form the centre word.

59: Figure A is the missing face, the one shaped like an upright capital N.

60: B. In each row and column, faces can have one of three shapes, three expressions, and three types of eye. Only B has all the features that are missing from the last row or column..

CHAPTER TWENTY-ONE

ANSWERS TO EXERCISE TESTS

NUMBERS QUIZ

Q29: 26. Double each term and add 2 to get the next one in the series.

Q30: 25 and 29. Steps across add 1 from left to right; steps down add 5.

Q31: 36. Add 2 and 10 alternately.

Q32: 14. The interval increases by 1 each time.

Q33: 23. Square the numbers 1,2,3,4,5 and subtract 2.

Q34: 55. Go clockwise, double each term and add 1.

Q35: 6. The numbers on the left-hand segments are three times those on the right. If you put 1, you deserve to lose a mark for being perverse!

Q36: 7 and 24. The top series progresses in steps of +1, −2, +3, and −4; the bottom series progresses by −1, +2, −3, and +4.

Q37: 21. Go round alternate segments anticlockwise, adding 2 each time.

Q38: 1. Add the squares of the numbers in the triangles to the number in the box to reach the number in the circle.

LETTERS AND NUMBERS QUIZ

Q63: 15. Vowels count 1, consonants count 2.

Q64: P. Go back in the alphabet five letters each time. Begin at J and start at Z again when you get to A.

Q65: S. The letters are the initials of the days of the week, starting with Sunday.

Q66: 6642. Each number indicates the number of places up or down the alphabet which you must skip in order to get the letter immediately below.

ANSWERS

Q67: BACK. Take the fourth and second letters of the first word and the first and third letters of the second.

Q68: 17 and E. The top row is a series of prime numbers – that is, numbers which cannot be divided by anything except themselves and 1. The bottom row is the letters which correspond to those positions in the alphabet — written backwards just to make it more difficult.

Q69: Y. Go forwards (or backwards) through the alphabet by the gap indicated by each number.

Q70: CELLOS and CHORAL. Translate the numbers attached to each letter in the word ORCHESTRAL (O=1, R=2, etc) to construct the two missing words.

Q71: 1 and X. There are two sequences. The numerical one falls by an interval that increases by 1 each time. The letter sequence has similarly increasing intervals, but going forwards.

Q72: E, B, M, T. The top row spells the word SENSIBLY, while the bottom row spells the word MARITIME. The domino layout is just there to confuse you.

WORDS QUIZ

Q89: NEW YORK. It is the only one which is not a capital city. (Only residents of New York State can be excused for getting this one wrong.)

Q90: OX. All the others can be prefixed by the word CAR.

Q91: LINE. The pronunciation of LINEAGE might mislead you on this one.

Q92: SMITH. This is a disguised letter question. The subjects begin with the letter two down the alphabet from the opening letter of the surnames, with this one exception..

Q93: CROSS. You might be too, if you didn't get that easy one.

Q94: CIRCLE. Start with the two-dimensional shape and raise it up into the third dimension.

Q95: ENTICE. Not INTRIGUE as many people presume.

Q96: CITY. All the other words can be used as either nouns or verbs.

Q97: RECEDE. Unlike DEPART, this does not presume any starting point, just as APPROACH does not presume any final point of contact.

Q98: LED. Were you fooled by HOLED?

VISUAL QUIZ

Q117: The remaining face shows a V on its side, so:

Q118: B. Remove the right-hand edge and replace it with a mirror-image of the remainder.

Q119: Four dots on the top and three on the bottom. Yes, it really is that straightforward, but you don't have much scope for fancy stunts in a dominoes question.

Q120: C. Take lines above the centre stroke to be +1, lines below to be –1, and add them up.

Q121: B. The fish move clockwise by one-quarter of a revolution in each row (or anticlockwise by one-eighth of a revolution in each column).

Q122: C. The number of lines increases by one each time. There is no other pattern.

Q123: C. Each can be divided symmetrically, with a dot in each half, except C.

Q124: C (again). The hatching pattern moves systematically down the figures.

Q125: 2 and 5.

Q126: 12 squares and 24 triangles.

LOGIC QUIZ

Q132: The answer is (b). Some others *may* be true, but not necessarily so.

Q133: Mary had a little lamb, its fleece was white as snow. X, E, B are not used.

Q134: I bought 24 plates.

Q135: Fifteen black tiles is the minimum.

Q136: 7.06.

Q137: Move the foresight to the left and down. Move the back-sight to the right and up. The only way to do this puzzle is to think of how you would have to adjust the sights for them to be focused on the spot which the gun actually hits! And that is how, in practice, you do adjust gun-sights.Thinking of moving the barrel up to the bull's-eye and then working out what you have to do to the sights in compensation will get you quickly tied up in mental knots!

CHAPTER TWENTY-TWO

ANSWERS TO TEST TWO

When checking your answers to this test, you might find that you have come up with an alternative answer and explanation that seems just as good as the ones given. You may count this as correct, provided that your reasoning could not lead to any other solution being correct, and is not unnecessarily convoluted as seen against a straightforward explanation.

When you have checked your answers, add up the number of correct solutions you obtained. You can translate your score into a rough estimate of your IQ using the chart on page 168.

1:     C. In each row and column, there is a circle, heart, or diamond; the right-hand section is black, white, or shaded; and the left-hand section contains one, two, or three stripes.

2:     TENT. Take the first and second letters of the right-hand word plus the first and last letters of the left-hand word to form the new word.

3:     9. There are two alternating series, one increasing by two each time, the other diminishing by one each time.

4:     ODE.

5:     A. The stripes increase in number right to left, and their rotation changes anticlockwise by forty-five degrees from one figure to the next.

6:     M and 6. The letters advance by three in the alphabetical series, and the numbers advance by three each time.

7:     6 and 10. The numbers increase in steps of two from left to right, and in steps of one from top to bottom.

8:     | 5 | 2 | The first box contains a series going up in singles; the second contains a diminishing series.

9:     S. The opposing words make the new words HEATHER, BONDAGE, CUPID, WALLPAPER, and PENSION.

10: 7. The numbers in the top are half those directly below in the bottom.

11: E and P. The letters make up the words TOP, ODE, and PEA in each direction.

12: KIND.

13 E. The dots sum across each row and each column.

14: 24. Vowels count 10, consonants 1.

15: WALL and WOW. The others are pairs of words which sound the same. Although WALL and WOW do rhyme with other words on the list, they start with a different sound.

16: 6. Add the first and second numbers in each box and add one to get the last figure.

17: WINE. Letters above are one behind in the alphabet, letters below are one further on.

18: The segments above the horizon contain the opposites of those below. The others are cat/dog, −3/+3, and happy/sad.

19: EAR. This makes the words SHEAR and EARTH.

20: C. The figures have 0, 1, 2, and 3 curved sides respectively.

21: OWL. Owls are birds, while all the others are mammals. Also, it is the only word where the vowel is not in the middle.

22: B. There are one, two, or three hearts, diamonds, or circles on each row and in each column.

23: Z. Following the alphabetical sequence, the interval between the letters increases by one each time.

24: D. A and E are identical, so are B and C.

25: BOW. It completes the first word to make RAINBOW and starts the second to make BOWLING.

26: R. The intervals between the letters are 5, 4, 3, 2, and 1.

27: 12. The rows and columns all sum to 24.

28: BALE. Take the fourth and first letters of the first word, then the fourth and first letters of the second word to form the word in the centre.

29: B. In each row and column, there are two circles, two squares, and two triangles, one at the top of a figure and one at the bottom.

30: 858. Add the numbers in the triangles and multiply the result by two.

31: 6. Divide the number in the diamond by the number in the triangle, and double the result.

32: VOLUME.

33: E. The flowers in each row and column are black, white, and speckled, so are the pots.

34: KARP, an anagram of PARK. All the others are anagrams of rooms: HALL, KITCHEN, BEDROOM, and ATTIC.

35: TRAM. Take the last and first letters of the first word, plus the third and first letters of the second, to form the new word.

36: 2.

37: 33. Add the upper numbers and multiply by three.

38: S. The series progresses, clockwise from A, through the alphabet in steps of three.

39: W. In the alphabetical series, the interval between the letters increases by one each time.

40: A and A. The back of the seat spells ARMCHAIR clockwise.

41: P. Take the squares of 5, 4, 3, 2, and 1, and translate them into their position in the alphabet.

42: B. The large figure is halved and changes colour. The small figure becomes smaller, rotates forty-five degrees, moves underneath, and changes colour.

43: ASLEEP. A physical state; the others are all character dispositions.

44: 32. Take the cubes of the five numbers on the left, and halve them.

45: D. Black dots count +1, white dots count –1, and the rows and columns sum.

46: 15 and 100. The intervals in the top row increase by one each time; the numbers in the bottom row are the squares of the top, in backwards order.

47: PUMMS, an anagram of MUMPS. All the others are anagrams of the names of domestic furniture items: WARDROBE, CHAIR, and TABLE.

48: T. The letters are the initial letters of the name of the first twelve numbers: one, two, three, four, and so on.

49: 1. Take the difference between the numbers in circles, and divide by the number in the square.

50: E. In each row and column, the circle contains a smile, frown, and blank; the upper box contains a triangle, ellipse, or circle; and the lower box contains a diagonal, a cross, or a blank.

51: 7. The ratio between the top numbers and those below them is 4:7 throughout.

52: B The words in each pair, taken together, sound like new words: BEETROOT and SUNDAYS.

53: F. The first and second elements of each pair have three different shapes and three different colorations, with no repeats in any row or column. F provides the missing combination of shapes and colours.

54: 22. Add the digits of the outer numbers to get the number in the box.

55: D. Repeating horizontals cancel, while dissimilar ones leave a horizontal in the third row and third column. Two upward or downward slopes sum to an upward slope in the third row and column, while opposites sum to a downward slope.

56: ATTUNED. The second and third letters of the others are consecutive in the alphabet.

57: FAST.

58: 18. The bottom numbers are twice the top row, plus 1, 2, 3, and 4.

59: P and S. The letters spell PLEASURE when read clockwise.

60: HEAL.

CHAPTER TWENTY-THREE

TRANSLATING YOUR SCORES INTO IQ

You can translate your scores on Test One and Test Two into rough estimates of your IQ by using the chart below.

However, when you do so, remember that these tests are meant primarily for fun and you should certainly not let your score on them influence any important decisions about your life or anyone else's. You need to take a series of professional IQ tests before you can approach a useful measure of your IQ — and as you know from reading this book, there is much more to human life and human abilities than IQ anyway!

In particular, the tests are not suitable for personnel selection or any other competitive situation. The tests are designed for application principally to educated Westerners, and people from different educational and cultural backgrounds may obtain very divergent scores on these tests.

To read the chart, look up the score you gave yourself on Test One or Test Two and trace it horizontally along to the black line. Trace vertically down from there to get a rough measure of your IQ. However, this is only a *rough* measure, and you could well be seven IQ-points either side of that figure when your IQ is measured professionally. We have indicated this range of error with the blocks on the graph. Happy testing!

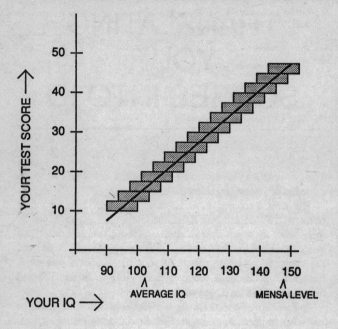